MICHAEL GRAVES

MICHAEL GRAVES
BUILDINGS AND PROJECTS
1966-1981

ESSAY by VINCENT SCULLY

EDITED
by
KAREN VOGEL WHEELER
PETER ARNELL
TED BICKFORD

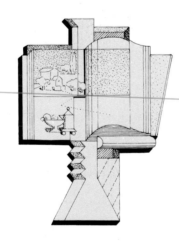

RIZZOLI
NEW YORK

First published in Great Britain in 1983 by
The Architectural Press Ltd.
9 Queen Anne's Gate, London SW1H 9BY

Published in the United States of America in 1982 by
Rizzoli International Publications, Inc.,
712 Fifth Avenue, New York, 10019

ISBN 0 85139 848 0

Lay-out by
Arnell / Bickford Associates, New York City

CONTENTS

Rome 1981

A CASE FOR FIGURATIVE ARCHITECTURE

By Michael Graves

A standard form and a poetic form exist in any language or in any art. Although analogies drawn between one cultural form and another prove somewhat difficult, they nevertheless allow associations that would otherwise be impossible. Literature is the cultural form which most obviously takes advantage of standard and poetic usages, and so may stand as a model for architectural dialogue. In literature, the standard, accessible, simple ranges of daily use are expressed in conversational or prose forms, while the poetic attitudes of language are used to test, deny, and at times, to further support standard language. It seems that standard language and poetic language have a reciprocal responsibility to stand as separate and equal strands of the greater literary form and to reinforce each other by their similarity and diversity. Through this relationship of tension, each form is held in check and plays on the other for its strength.

When applying this distinction of language to architecture, it could be said that the standard form of building is its common or internal language. The term internal language does not imply in this case that it is non-accessible, but rather that it is intrinsic to building in its most basic form—determined by pragmatic, constructional, and technical requirements. In contrast, the poetic form of architecture is responsive to issues external to the building, and incorporates the three-dimensional expression of the myths and rituals of society. Poetic forms in architecture are sensitive to the figurative, associative, and anthropomorphic attitudes of a culture. If one's goal is to build with only utility in mind, then it is enough to be conscious of technical criteria alone. However, once aware of and responsive to the possible cultural influences on building, it is important that society's patterns of ritual be registered in the architecture. Could these two attitudes, one technical and utilitarian and the other cultural and symbolic, be thought of as architecture's standard and poetic languages?

Without doubt, the inevitable overlap of these two systems of thought can cause this argument to become somewhat equivocal. However, the salient tendencies of each attitude may be distinguished and reasonably discussed. This is said with some critical knowledge of the recent past. It could be maintained that dominant aspects of modern architecture were formulated without this debate about standard and poetic language, or internal and external manifestations of architectural culture. The Modern Movement based itself largely on technical expression—internal language—and the metaphor of the machine dominated its building form. In its rejection of the human or anthropomorphic representation of previous architecture, the Modern Movement undermined the poetic form in favor of

nonfigural, abstract geometries. These abstract geometrics might in part have been derived from the simple internal forms of machines themselves. Coincident with machine metaphors in buildings, architecture in the first half of this century also embraced aesthetic abstraction in general. This has contributed to our interest in purposeful ambiguity, the possibility of double readings within compositions.

While any architectural language, to be built, will always exist within the technical realm, it is important to keep the technical expression parallel to an equal and complementary expression of ritual and symbol. It could be argued that the Modern Movement did this, that as well as its internal language, it expressed the symbol of the machine, and therefore practiced cultural symbolism. But in this case, the machine is retroactive, for the machine itself is a utility. So this symbol is not an external allusion, but rather a second, internalized reading. A significant architecture must incorporate both internal and external expressions. The external language, which engages inventions of culture at large, is rooted in a figurative, associational and anthropomorphic attitude.

We assume that in any construct, architectural or otherwise, technique, the art of making something, will always play a role. However, it should also be said that the components of architecture have not only derived from pragmatic necessity, but also evolved from symbolic sources. Architectural elements are recognized for their symbolic aspect and used metaphorically by other disciplines. A novelist, for example, will stand his character next to a window and use the window as a frame through which we read or understand the character's attitude and position.

In architecture, however, where they are attendant to physical structure, basic elements are more frequently taken for granted. In this context, the elements can become so familiar that they are not missed when they are eliminated or when they are used in a slang version. For instance, if we imagine ourselves standing adjacent to a window, we expect the window sill to be somehow coincident with the waist of our body. We also expect, or might reasonably ask, that its frame help us make sense not only of the landscape beyond, but also of our own position relative to the geometry of the window and to the building as a whole. In modern architecture, however, these expectations are seldom met, and instead the window is often continuous with the wall as horizontal banding or, more alarmingly, it becomes the entire surface. The naming of the "window wall" is a prime example of the conflation or confusion of architectural elements.

Architectural elements require this distinction, one from another, in much the same way as language requires syntax; without variations among architectural elements, we will lose the anthropomorphic or figurative meaning. The elements of any enclosure include wall, floor, ceiling, column, door, and window. It might be wondered why these elements, given their geometric similarity in some cases (for example, floor and ceiling) must be understood differently. It is essential in any symbolic construct to identify the thematic differences between various parts of the whole. If the floor as ground is regarded as distinct from the soffit as sky, then the material, textural, chromatic, and decorative inferences are dramatically different. Yet in a formal sense, these are both horizontal planes.

We as architects must be aware of the difficulties and the strengths of thematic and figural aspects of the work. If the external aspects of the composition, that part of our language which extends beyond internal technical requirements, can be thought of as the resonance of man and nature, we quickly sense an historical pattern of external language. All architecture before the Modern Movement sought to elaborate the themes of man and landscape. Understanding the building involves both association with natural phenomena (for example, the ground is like the floor), and anthropomorphic allusions (for example, a column is like a man). These two attitudes within the symbolic nature of building were probably originally in part ways of justifying the elements of architecture in a prescientific society. However, even today, the same metaphors are required for access to our own myths and rituals within the building narrative.

Although there are, of course, instances where the technical assemblage of buildings employs metaphors and forms from nature, there is also possibility for a larger, external natural text within the building narrative. The suggestion that the soffit is in some sense celestial, is certainly our cultural invention, and it becomes increasingly interesting as other elements of the building also reinforce such a narrative. This type of cultural association allows us "into" the full text or language of the architecture. This is in contrast to modern examples which commonly sacrifice the idea or theme in favor of a more abstract language. In these instances, the composition, while perhaps formally satisfying, is based only on internal references. A de Stijl composition is as satisfying turned upside down as it is right side up, and this is in part where its interest lies. We may admire it for its compositional unity, but as architecture, because of its lack of interest in nature and gravity, it dwells outside the reference systems of architectural themes. A de Stijl building has two internal systems, one technical and the other abstract.

In making a case for figurative architecture, we assume that the thematic character of the work is grounded in nature and is simultaneously read in a totemic or anthropomorphic manner. An example of this double reading might be had by analyzing the character of a wall. As the window helps us to understand our size and presence within the room, so the wall, though more abstract as a geometric plane, has over time accommodated both pragmatic and symbolic divisions. Once the wainscot or chair rail is understood as being similar in height to the window sill, associations between the base of the wall (which that division provides) and our own bodies are easily made. As we stand upright and are, in a sense, rooted in the ground, so the wall, through its wainscot division, is rooted relative to the floor. Another horizontal division takes place at the pic-

ture molding, where the soffit is dropped from its horizontal position to a linear division at the upper reaches of the wall. Although this tripartite division of the wall into base, body, and head does not literally imitate man, it nevertheless stabilizes the wall relative to the room, an effect we take for granted in our bodily presence there.

The mimetic character that a wall offers the room, as the basic substance of its enclosure, is obviously distinct from the plan of the room. While we see and understand the wall in a face to face manner, we stand perpendicular to the plan. The wall contributes primarily to the character of the room because of its figurative possibilities. The plan, however, because it is seen perspectively, is less capable of expressing character and more involved with our spatial understanding of the room. While space can be appreciated on its own terms as amorphous, it is ultimately desirable to create a reciprocity between wall and plan, where the wall surfaces or enclosures are drawn taut around a spatial idea. The reciprocity of plan and wall is finally more interesting than the distinctions between them.

We can say that both wall and plan have a center and edges. The plan alone, however, has no top, middle and base, as does the wall. At this point, we must rely on the reciprocal action or volumetric continuity provided by both. Understanding that it is the volumetric idea that will be ultimately considered, we can analyze, with some isolation, how the plan itself contributes to a figurative architectural language.

For the purposes of this argument, a linear plan, three times as long as it is wide, might be compared to a square or centroidal plan. The square plan provides an obvious center, and at the same time, emphasizes its edges or periphery. If the square plan is further divided, like tic-tac-toe, into nine squares, the result is an even greater definition of corners, edges, and a single center. If we continue to elaborate such a geometric proposition with freestanding artifacts such as furniture, the locations of tables and chairs will be not only pragmatic, but also symbolic of societal interactions. One can envision many compositions and configurations of the same pieces of furniture which would offer us different meanings within the room.

Predictably, the three square composition will subdivide quite differently from the centroidal plan. While the rectangular composition will distinguish the middle third of the room as its center, and the outer thirds as its flanks, we are less conscious here of occupiable corners. The corners of the square composition contribute to our understanding of the center and are read as positive. In contrast, the corners of the rectangular plan are remote from its center and are seemingly residual. Our culture understands the geometric center as special and as the place of primary human occupation. We would not typically divide the rectangular room into two halves, but rather, more appropriately, would tend to place ourselves in the center, thereby precluding any reading of the room as a diptych. In analyzing room configurations, we sense a cultural bias to certain basic geometries. We habitually see ourselves, if not at the center of our "universe", at least at the center of the spaces we occupy. This assumption colors our understanding of the differences between center and edge.

If we compare the understanding of the exterior of the building to that of its interior volume, another dimension of figurative architecture arises. A freestanding building such as Palladio's Villa Rotunda, is comprehensible in its object-hood. Furthermore, its interior volume can be read similarly—not as a figural object, but as a figural void. A comparison between such an ''object building'' and a building of the Modern Movement, such as Mies van der Rohe's Barcelona Pavilion, allows us to see how the abstract character of space in Mies's building dissolves any reference to or understanding of figural void or space. We cannot charge Mies with failing to offer us figurative architecture, for this is clearly not his intention. However, we can say that, without the sense of enclosure that the Palladio example offers us, we have a much thinner palette than if we allow the possibility of both the ephemeral space of modern architecture and the enclosure of traditional architecture. It could be contended that amorphic or continuous space, as understood in the Barcelona Pavilion, is oblivious to bodily or totemic reference, and we therefore always find ourselves unable to feel centered in such space. This lack of figural reference ultimately contributes to a feeling of alienation in buildings based on such singular propositions.

In this discussion of wall and plan, an argument is made for the figural necessity of each particular element and, by extension, of architecture as a whole. While certain monuments of the Modern Movement have introduced new spatial configurations, the cumulative effect of non-figurative architecture is the dismemberment of our former cultural language of architecture. This is not so much an historical problem as it is one of a cultural continuum. It may be glib to suggest that the Modern Movement be seen not so much as an historical break but as an appendage to the basic and continuing figurative mode of expression. However, it is nevertheless crucial that we re-establish the thematic associations invented by our culture in order to fully allow the culture of architecture to represent the mythic and ritual aspirations of society.

Michael Graves,
January 1982

PROJECT ASSISTANTS 1966-1981

The following people have worked in Michael Graves' office and have contributed to the projects shown here.

BRUCE ABBEY — CLARA DA CRUZ ALMEIDA — BERNARD ALTHABEGOITY — PETER ARNELL — KENNETH BEHLES — CHRISTOPHER BENE — RONALD BERLIN — TED BICKFORD — THEODORE BROWN — C. J. CANTWELL — PETER CARL — ELLEN CHENG — CHRISTOPHER CHIMERA — MARK CIGOLLE — LINDA JOY COHEN — CAROLINE CONSTANT — STEPHEN CORELLI — DENNIS CORMIER — ROGER CROWLEY — DOUGLAS ELY — MICHAEL FAREWELL — PATRICIA FINGERHOOD — LAUREL FITCH — YOSSI FRIEDMAN — PIERRE FUHRER — WANATHA GARNER — MADLEN GOLDSTINE — NICHOLAS GONSER — JOSE GONZALEZ BARAHONA — RUTH GOODMAN — GAIL GRAVES — STAN HAAS — LAWRENCE HAINES — JULIE HANSELMANN — STEVEN HARRIS — GAVIN HOGBEN — JANE KENT — RANDALL KORMAN — BENJAMIN KRACAUER — ERIC KUHNE — CHARLES LAGRECO — LISA LEE — DIANE LEGGE — NANCY CONN LEVIN — STEPHEN LEVINE — PETER LOKHAMMER — BRUCE MACNELLY — JOSEPH MANCUSO — RONALD McCOY — LAURIN McCRAKEN — PEDRO MENDOZA — PETER MICKLE — BRUCE MILLER — ANAEZI MODU — MIMI MORTON — DEBORAH NATSIOS — THOMAS NAVIN — ROBERT NICHOLS — SHARON PACHTER — DOUGLASS PASCHALL — CLEMENT PAULSEN — MASON PERKINS — STEPHEN PERKINS — G. DANIEL PERRY — THOMAS PRITCHARD — DAVID READING — PAUL ROBERTSON — DAVID ROCKWOOD — NONYA SCHWARTZ — MASAHARU SENO — GORDON SMITH — JULIET RICHARDSON SMITH — SYLVIA SMITH — TERENCE SMITH — HENRY SMITH-MILLER — SUZANNE STRUM — JAMES SWAN — THOMAS SZUMLICZ — KEAT TAN — WILLIAM TAYLOR — DAVID TEETERS — SARA JANE TSAKONAS — PETER TWOMBLY — MAX UNDERWOOD — SUZANNE KOLARIK UNDERWOOD — RONALD VANARD — PETER WALDMAN — GLORIA WALTERS — SETH WARNER — BARBARA VAN DER WEE — KAREN VOGEL WHEELER — ROBERT CAREY WHITE — BRIAN WISHNE — GARY WOLF — TIMOTHY WOOD — KONRAD WOS — DAVID ZUNG

INDEX

1967

Hanselmann House
Fort Wayne, Indiana

View from the street

This house for a family of two adults and four children is located on a corner site which is entered adjacent to a stream running diagonally through the property. The house and the space immediately in front of it make a double square in plan and volumetrically a double cube, with one being open and the other enclosed. The house is understood frontally by the layering of three principal facades. The first of these, consisting of a pipe rail frame and the front plane of a studio house (which have not been built), defines the outer edge of the house's precinct. It acts as a gate, receiving the stair between the ground and the entrance level. The main volume of the house is entered through the second primary facade, located at the center of the composition. This point of entry is also reflected in the distortion of the plan of the roof terrace above. The third facade, which is the densest, is the rear wall of the house containing the mural. The imagery of the mural identifies elements of the house's composition and the surrounding landscape. An outdoor terrace on the ground level relates to the diagonal of the stream and implies a larger compositional frame in which the idealized geometry of the house is seen in opposition to the natural landscape.

Hanselmann House

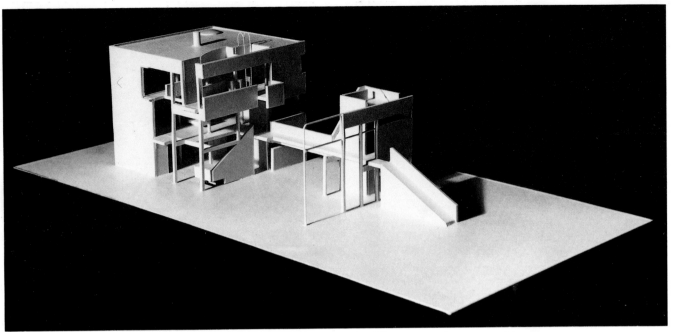

Southwest view of model

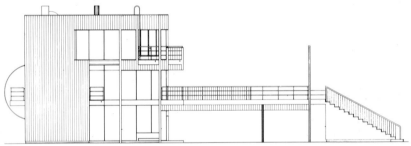

South elevation

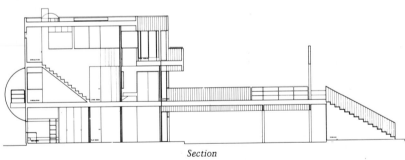

Section

Southwest corner

Southwest corner

Hanselmann House

Living room interior

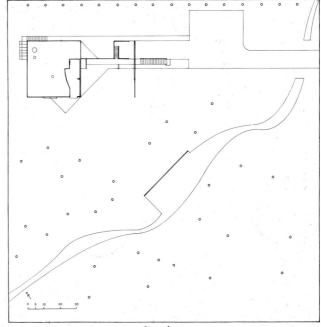

Site plan

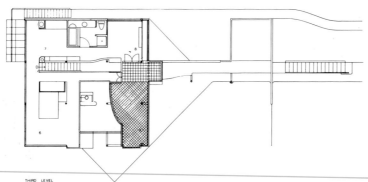

THIRD LEVEL

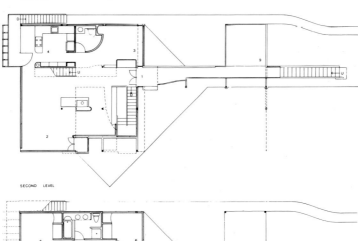

SECOND LEVEL

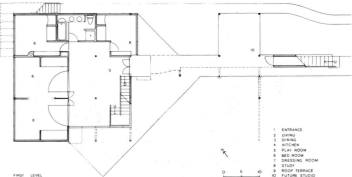

FIRST LEVEL

1 ENTRANCE
2 LIVING
3 DINING
4 KITCHEN
5 PLAY ROOM
6 BED ROOM
7 DRESSING ROOM
8 STUDY
9 ROOF TERRACE
10 FUTURE STUDIO

0 5 10

21

Entrance facade

First floor entrance

Dining room wall detail

Living room with mural

Interior view of third level

1966

Oyster Bay Town Plan
Oyster Bay, New York

Overhead view of model

The town of Oyster Bay is sited on a plain between a range of hills on one side and Oyster Bay Harbor and Long Island Sound on the other. As the town grew, it turned its back on the two natural boundaries of water and hill and became an introverted community. In this project, current land uses were evaluated and reassessed, and an overall plan was made to restore the urban and recreational potential to the community by eliminating the isolation caused by the town's introverted growth.

A spur of the Long Island Railroad separates the town center from the public beach, harbor, and the Theodore Roosevelt Memorial Park, the community's primary recreational facilities. The design proposal truncates the railroad line to allow freer access to recreation areas and reorganizes pedestrian and vehicular movement patterns to encourage the urban interaction necessary for the economic growth of the commercial center. The overall plan also provides an organization for the location and growth of urban institutions, including public school expansion, a junior college level technical institute, cultural facilities, and new entertainment facilities.

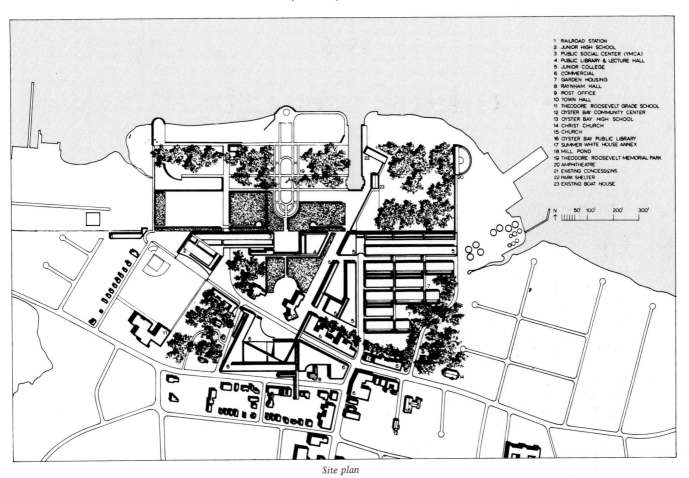

1 RAILROAD STATION
2 JUNIOR HIGH SCHOOL
3 PUBLIC SOCIAL CENTER (YMCA)
4 PUBLIC LIBRARY & LECTURE HALL
5 JUNIOR COLLEGE
6 COMMERCIAL
7 GARDEN HOUSING
8 RAYNHAM HALL
9 POST OFFICE
10 TOWN HALL
11 THEODORE ROOSEVELT GRADE SCHOOL
12 OYSTER BAY COMMUNITY CENTER
13 OYSTER BAY HIGH SCHOOL
14 CHRIST CHURCH
15 CHURCH
16 OYSTER BAY PUBLIC LIBRARY
17 SUMMER WHITE HOUSE ANNEX
18 MILL POND
19 THEODORE ROOSEVELT MEMORIAL PARK
20 AMPHITHEATRE
21 EXISTING CONCESSIONS
22 PARK SHELTER
23 EXISTING BOAT HOUSE

Site plan

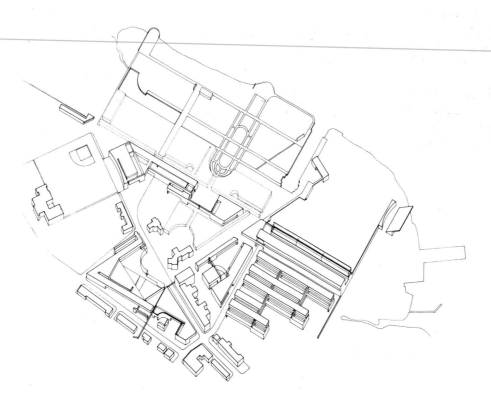

Site plan axonometric

1967

Union County Nature and Science Museum
Mountainside, New Jersey

Garden facade

This museum in the Watchung Mountains of northern New Jersey was intended to house exhibitions of local flora and fauna. Its program includes a lecture room, amphitheater, greenhouse, and exhibition space for permanent and changing installations. The building is organized in several zones, progressing from the enclosed lecture room for visitor orientation near the entrance, to more open exhibition space, to the semienclosed open-air amphitheater (not built), and finally to the park-like setting of the reservation in which the museum is located. Sequential layers, corresponding to the structural grid, frame views to the landscape which gradually become more open as one moves toward the outdoors. This serial, scenographic organization also allows future additions to the building to continue the architectural promenade.

Second floor balcony

Garden wall detail   *Upper floor walkway*   *Entry wall detail*

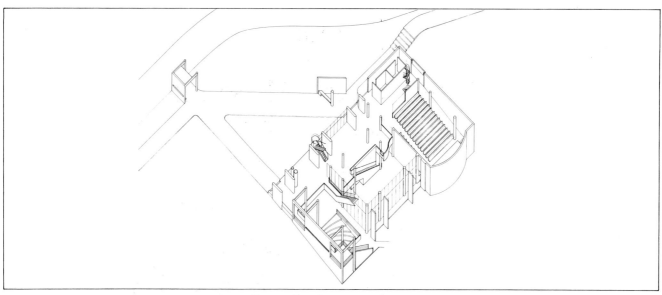

Entrance floor plan axonometric

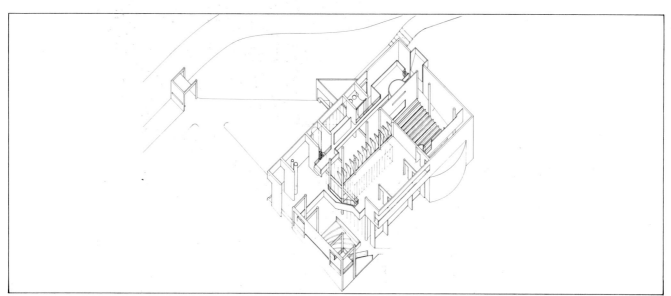

Upper floor plan axonometric

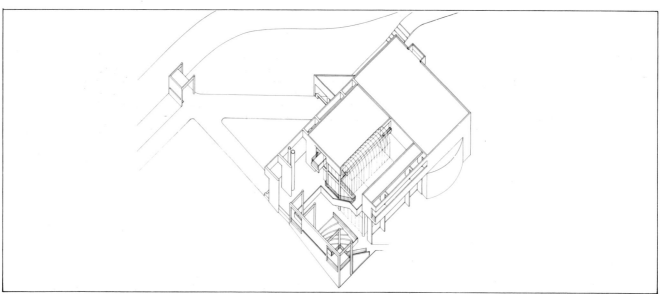

Roof plan axonometric

1968

The Newark Museum
Master Plan
Newark, New Jersey

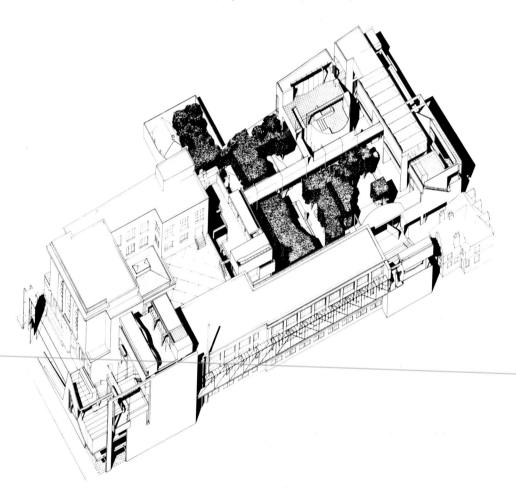

The master plan for the Newark Museum assembles into a unified whole the disparate existing facilities and historically significant buildings on the museum's complicated urban site. Included in the program are new gallery spaces, administrative offices, and an amphitheater for outdoor concerts. The existing buildings are organized by the new construction which consists of a series of linked pavilions surrounding the sculpture garden. The garden is thought of as an outdoor room containing artifacts such as large scale sculpture. Places for individual, casual visits are provided, along with more formal areas for group gatherings and performances.

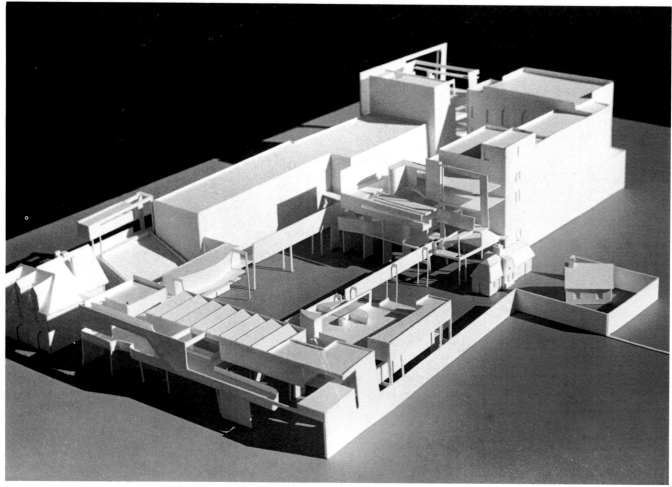

Southwest view of model

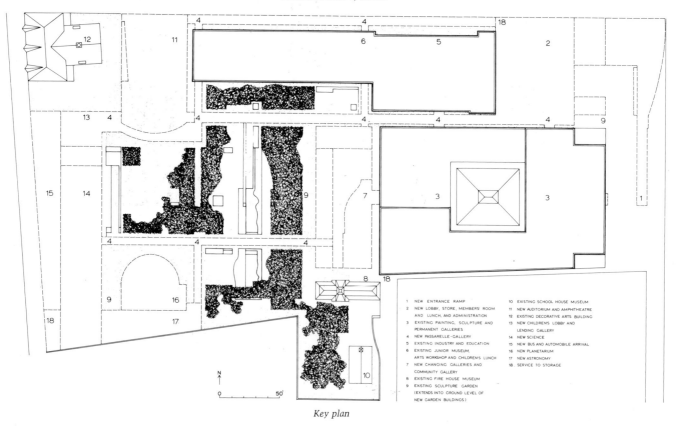

1 NEW ENTRANCE RAMP
2 NEW LOBBY, STORE, MEMBERS' ROOM AND LUNCH, AND ADMINISTRATION
3 EXISTING PAINTING, SCULPTURE AND PERMANENT GALLERIES
4 NEW PASSARELLE-GALLERY
5 EXISTING INDUSTRY AND EDUCATION
6 EXISTING JUNIOR MUSEUM, ARTS WORKSHOP AND CHILDREN'S LUNCH
7 NEW CHANGING GALLERIES AND COMMUNITY GALLERY
8 EXISTING FIRE HOUSE MUSEUM
9 EXISTING SCULPTURE GARDEN (EXTENDS INTO GROUND LEVEL OF NEW GARDEN BUILDINGS)

10 EXISTING SCHOOL HOUSE MUSEUM
11 NEW AUDITORIUM AND AMPHITHEATRE
12 EXISTING DECORATIVE ARTS BUILDING
13 NEW CHILDREN'S LOBBY AND LENDING GALLERY
14 NEW SCIENCE
15 NEW BUS AND AUTOMOBILE ARRIVAL
16 NEW PLANETARIUM
17 NEW ASTRONOMY
18 SERVICE TO STORAGE

N

0   50'

Key plan

1969

Benacerraf House
Princeton, New Jersey

Stair to roof terrace

The Benacerraf House addition was intended both as a free-standing pavilion in the garden and as an extension of the living spaces of the original house. The new composition terminates the existing main axis from the street as it turns toward the garden and the preferred light. The south facade, now primary, articulates a dialogue between nature and man-made artifact that is both actual and metaphorical. It acts as a sunscreen for the addition's roof terrace and at the same time, through the lyrical, curvilinear profile of its opening, reinterprets characteristics found in nature. The opening frames the view to the garden and the sky and can be seen as a representation of a treeline or clouds. On the same facade, the beam which supports the second story is equivalent in height to a hedgerow along the south border of the garden; painted green, the beam implies an association with the hedge in order to engage the space held between the two.

View from garden

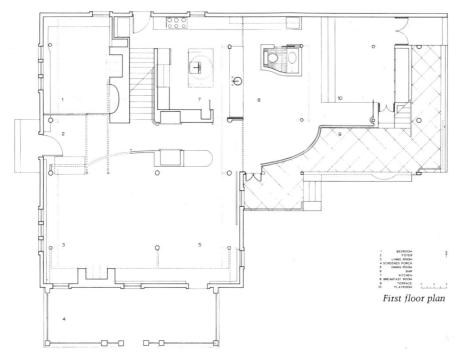

1	BEDROOM
2	FOYER
3	LIVING ROOM
4	SCREENED PORCH
5	DINING ROOM
6	BAR
7	KITCHEN
8	BREAKFAST ROOM
9	TERRACE
10	PLAYROOM

First floor plan

Garden facade

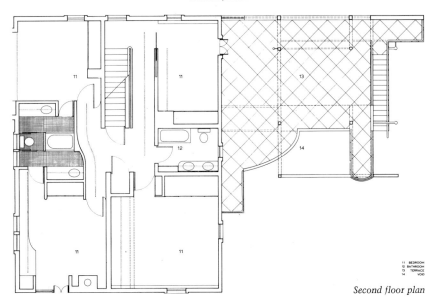

11 BEDROOM
12 BATHROOM
13 TERRACE
14 VOID

Second floor plan

Roof terrace balcony

Roof terrace

South facade

East facade

Roof terrace detail

Roof terrace detail

Roof terrace detail

First floor terrace detail

1969

Rockefeller House
Pocantico Hills, New York

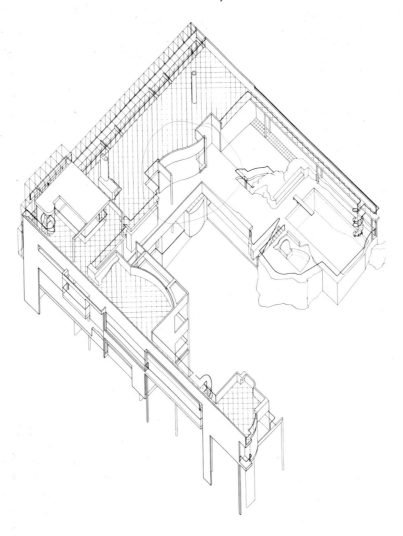

The Rockefeller House was designed as a residence for a family of six on a steeply sloping site with a distant view to the Hudson River. The house was to include separate bedrooms for four children, maids' quarters, guest room, swimming pool, and large recreation areas within the immediate grounds of the house.

The building is organized so that the driveway passes through the west facade into the precinct of the house and ascends to the entrance at the high point of the site. Family areas are located on the entrance level and bedrooms on the ground level below. Both the roof and the ground have been developed as terraces for outdoor social events.

In the composition, the landscape and the building are treated as interacting forces. The west facade serves as a datum for an actual and conceptual interdependency of house and site. As the entry facade, it marks the edge of the domain of the house and implies a building mass behind it into which natural elements, such as the figural void of the enclosed court, the pool, and the rock outcropping are seen to intrude. The guest pavilion has in turn been pulled away from the mass of the house, assuring the privacy and separateness which this element requires. Lyrical, freely disposed elements within the plan represent, on a metaphorical level, the introduction of nature into the rational grid of the house.

West view of model

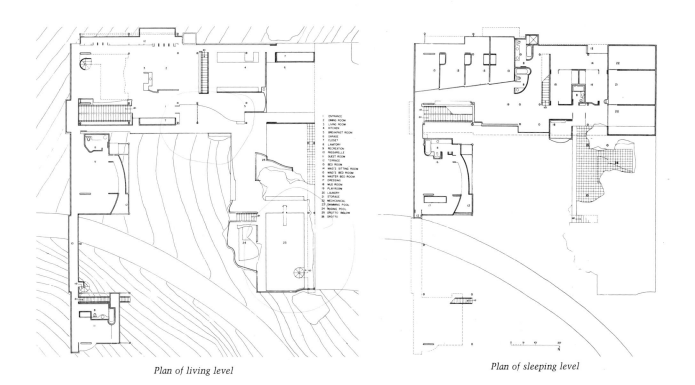

1 ENTRANCE
2 DINING ROOM
3 LIVING ROOM
4 KITCHEN
5 BREAKFAST ROOM
6 GARAGE
7 CLOSET
8 LAVATORY
9 RECREATION
10 PASSARELLE
11 GUEST ROOM
12 TERRACE
13 BED ROOM
14 MAID'S SITTING ROOM
15 MAID'S BED ROOM
16 MASTER BED ROOM
17 DRESSING
18 MUD ROOM
19 PLAY ROOM
20 LAUNDRY
21 STORAGE
22 MECHANICAL
23 SWIMMING POOL
24 WADING POOL
25 GROTTO BELOW
26 GROTTO

Plan of living level   *Plan of sleeping level*

Overhead view of model

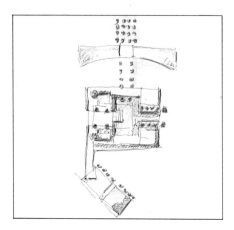

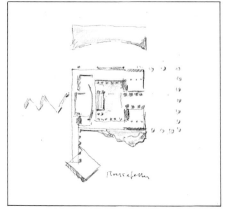

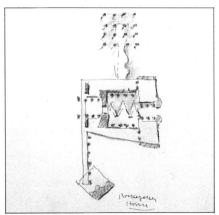

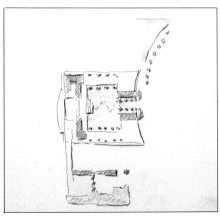

Preliminary studies

1970

Drezner House
Princeton, New Jersey

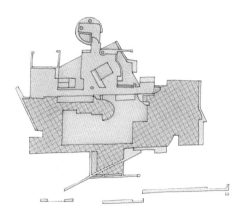

Second floor plan study

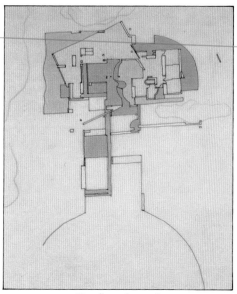

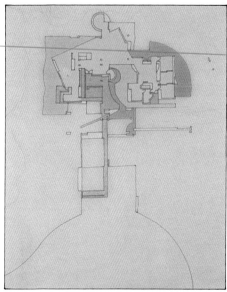

First floor plan study   *First floor plan study*

The site for the Drezner House is located at the end of a residential cul de sac. From the point of entry, two site influences are registered in the plan. One is a projection of one's frontal orientation to the site through the house to the private garden beyond, and the other, at an oblique angle to the first, refers to an existing clearing which is the most significant element of the otherwise densely wooded site. These two gestures are understood in the plan through their mutual influences which produce a spatial transparency where they are superimposed.

1973

Mezzo House
Princeton, New Jersey

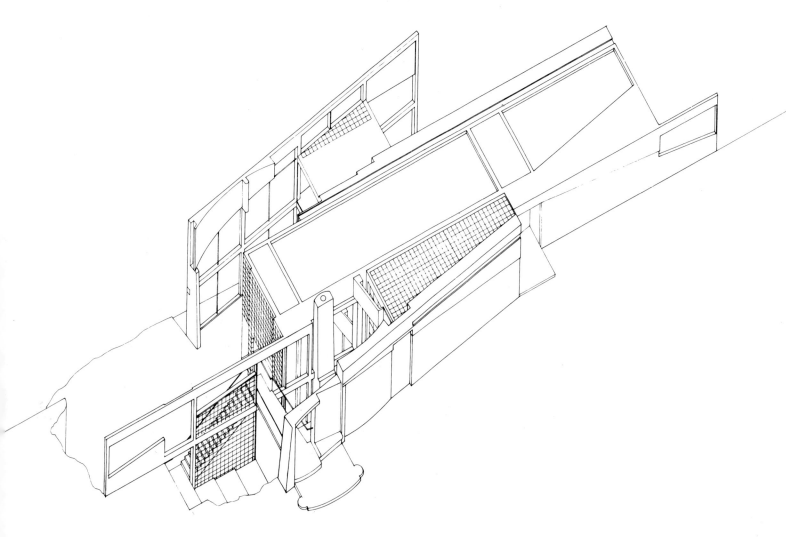

The Mezzo House is located on a steeply sloped site, entered at an upper level from the street and progressing downhill to a stream. The clients required that the major living areas be located on the lowest level, most removed from the street and therefore most private. In order to establish the "door" at this level, adjacent to the kitchen and social sections of the house, an exterior stair was located at one end of the scheme, thus bypassing the upper level bedrooms and more private activities of the house without bisecting the plan.

If the stairway is assumed to retain its classical role as a centralizing motif, the landscape can be seen in equity with the house itself. The oblique orientation of the slope relative to the street implies an enclosing gesture toward the garden and produces a means to identify the house with a broader landscape by drawing the adjacent site into the composition.

Mezzo House

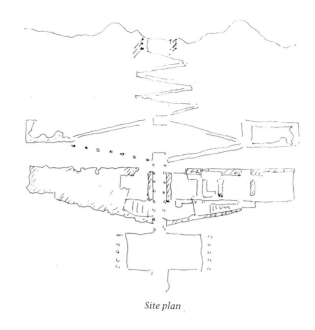

Site plan

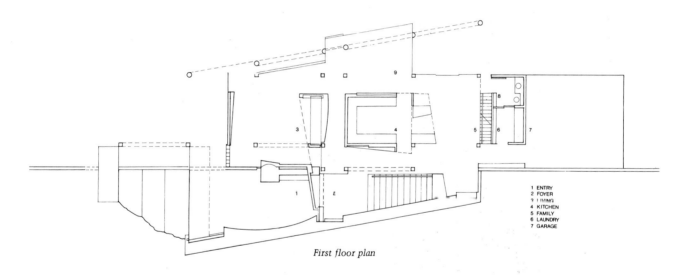

1 ENTRY
2 FOYER
3 LIVING
4 KITCHEN
5 FAMILY
6 LAUNDRY
7 GARAGE

First floor plan

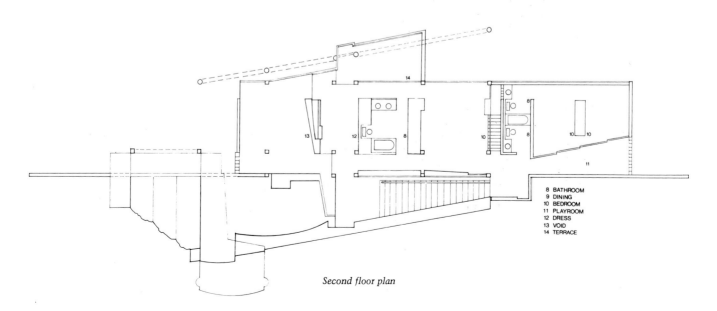

8 BATHROOM
9 DINING
10 BEDROOM
11 PLAYROOM
12 DRESS
13 VOID
14 TERRACE

Second floor plan

1971

Medical Office
Ear, Nose and Throat Associates
Fort Wayne, Indiana

Examining room

In this project, a single open space on the ground floor of a 1920's office building in Fort Wayne has been renovated for a medical group. The space, which is eleven feet high, has been subdivided by a series of lower, linked pavilions. The eight-foot height of these pavilions allows the large space, with its regular, gridded lighting, to be seen as continuous while providing smaller, more intimate rooms for particular functions such as reception, examining rooms, and doctors' offices.

The patient's path through the office is a circular progression from the entry and waiting area to the examination and treatment center and back, past scheduling and bookkeeping. The treatment center, with the examining rooms grouped around a central nurses' station, is rotated in plan to emphasize its programmatic importance. Each of the examining rooms is completely enclosed to provide acoustical separation from the main space, while the skylights in their ceilings allow a sense of the space beyond. Murals are located in each of the examining rooms and in a curving alcove opposite the nurses' station. In their window-like framing devices and abstracted allusions to the landscape, the murals visually extend the interior spaces.

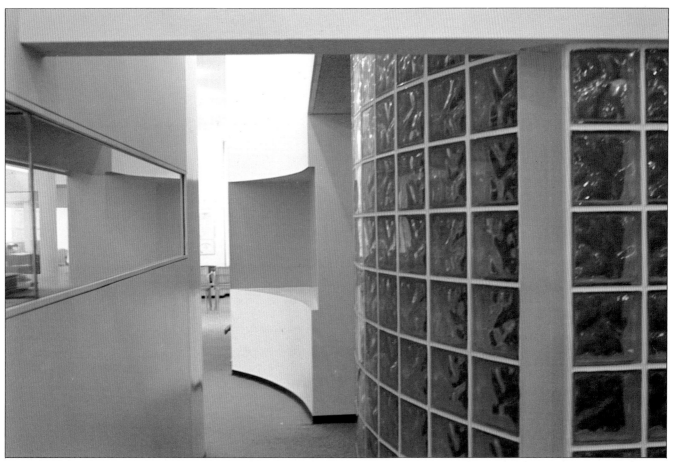

Office wall detail

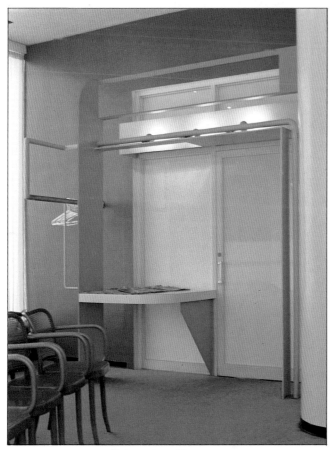

Entrance to waiting room

Examining room

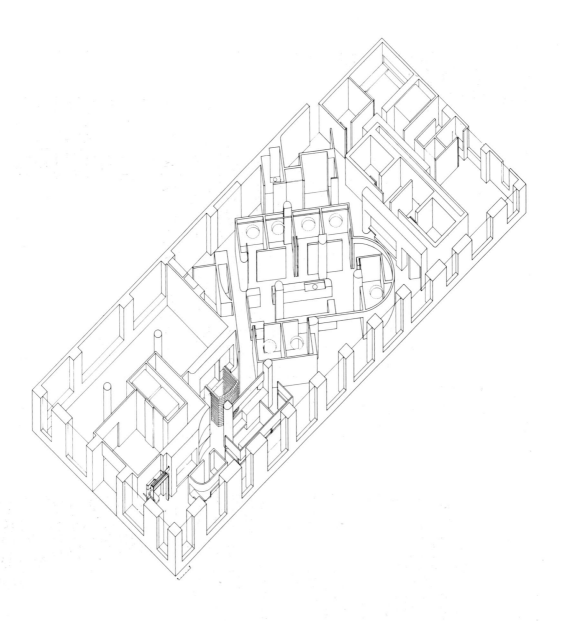

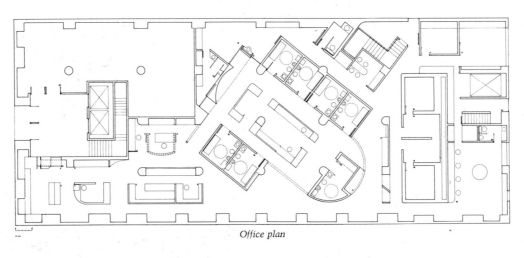

Office plan

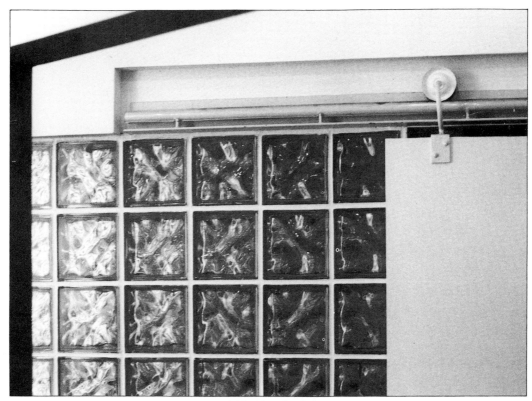

Sliding door detail

Passage to examining rooms

Reception

Nurses' station mural and examining room

Nurses' station mural

Nurses' station mural

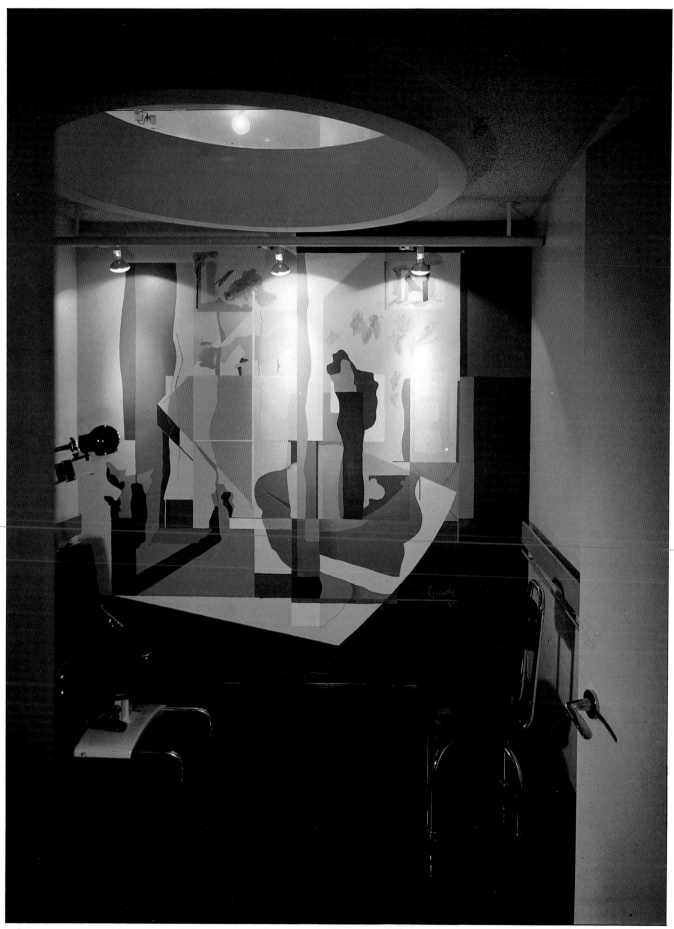

Examining room

1972

Keeley Guest House
Princeton, New Jersey

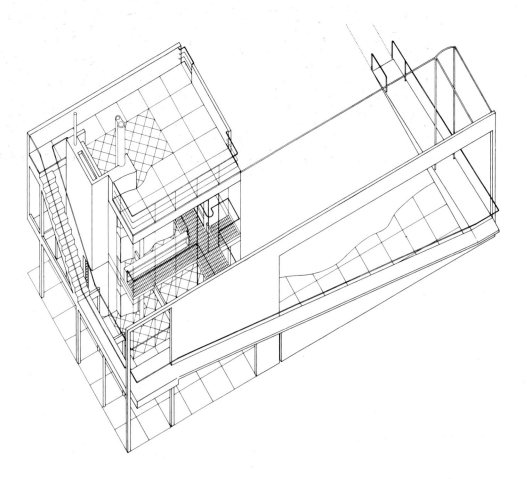

This addition, located on the garden side of an existing house, contains a writer's studio and a guest room for a university professor and his wife. It is intended to be both a free-standing pavilion in the garden and a logical extension of the original house. The studio is located at the ground level in order to place it in the garden, and is connected to the main house by a covered walkway, allowing it to be a direct extension of the social spaces of the house. The guest room is made more private by its location on the second floor. The third level terrace is to be used for sunning.

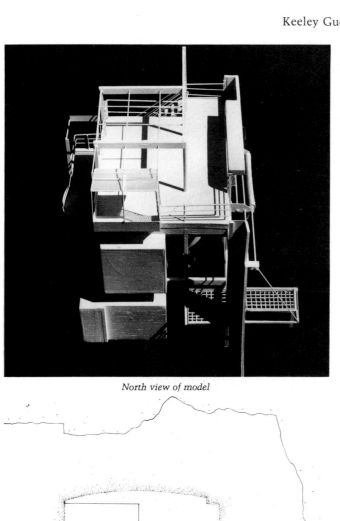

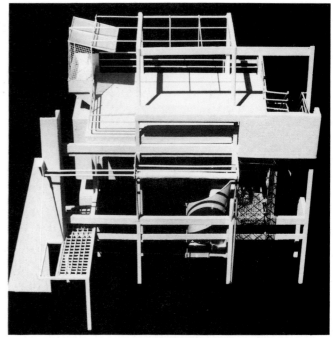

North view of model

West view of model

Second floor plan

Site plan

First floor plan

East view of model

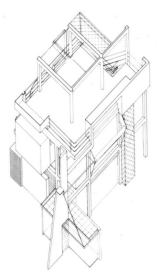

Preliminary axonometric

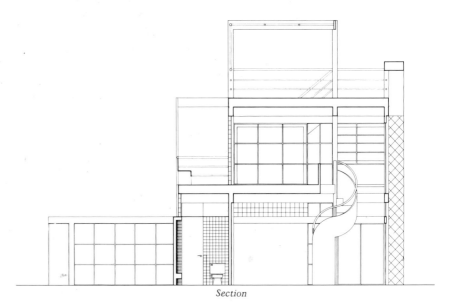

Section

1972

Snyderman House
Fort Wayne, Indiana

South facade

The Snyderman House is located on a heavily wooded forty acre site in Fort Wayne. The site is distinguished by a pond and a flat plateau opposite each other on an axis perpendicular to the natural entrance to the area. The house stands in a clearing at the intersection of these two axes, with the main entrance occurring on the east facade.

The program provides for a private residence for a family of six. The children's rooms on the second floor were designed to convert to a guest suite in the future. The plan is composed in four quadrants. The main stair occurs at the intersection of the two axes, just as the house itself occupies this special position in relation to the larger site. Within the plan, the rooms are organized both to take advantage of the appropriate exposure to the sun and to establish a progression from the entrance to the most private spaces. By its east-west alignment, the building, as man-made, is put in an ideal position in relation to the sun whose path from the front facade to the back traces both the course of a day's activities in the rooms and the movement from collective to more individual, private spaces.

Throughout the design, there is an interaction of opposed elements—flat and curved, interior and exterior, public and private—which is derived from an understanding of the house in its natural setting. The interaction between man-made and natural occurs at a metaphorical level and also permeates the built composition. The 'natural' is taken to mean that which shows the attributes of nature—irregularity, lyricism, movement. Similarly, 'man-made' becomes synonymous with idealized form, geometry, stasis. The curved forms of the guest suite and its oblique orientation, for instance, are seen in opposition to the idealized square of the house, in keeping with its programmatic separateness.

The polychromy is used to refer to both natural and man-made elements; color changes in the facades follow a logic consistent with the themes of the design. The colors are used to modify the perfection assumed in the white frame and to make allusions to elements found in the adjacent landscape.

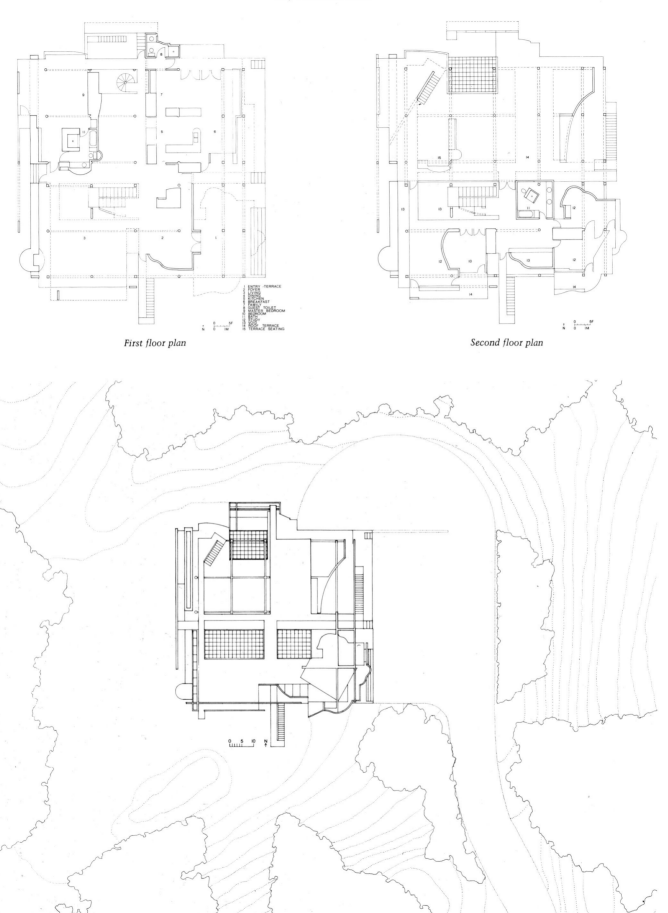

1 ENTRY · TERRACE
2 FOYER
3 LIVING
4 DINING
5 KITCHEN
6 BREAKFAST
7 FAMILY
8 GUEST · TOILET
9 MASTER · BEDROOM
10 BEDROOM
11 BATH
12 STUDY
13 VOID
14 ROOF · TERRACE
15 TERRACE · SEATING

First floor plan

Second floor plan

Site plan

Snyderman House

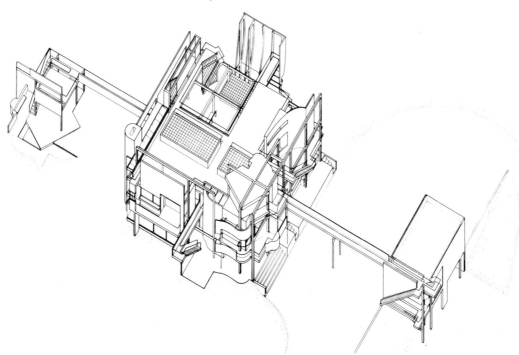

Axonometric of preliminary scheme

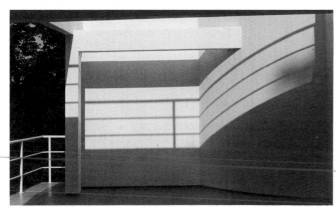

Roof terrace

Roof terrace balcony

Roof terrace

Oblique view of east facade

Guest room balcony

Entrance

East facade

Northeast corner

Southwest corner

South facade detail

South facade detail

Snyderman House

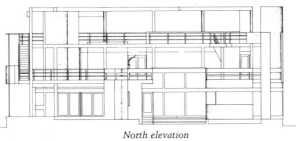

North elevation

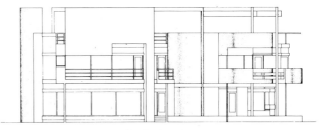

South elevation

Roof terrace stair

Staircase

Staircase

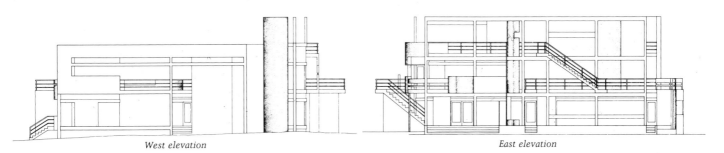

West elevation

East elevation

Staircase

Interior view looking south

Dining room

Living room

View of stair from living room

Dining room with mural

View of stair from second floor

1972

Professional Office
Gunwyn Ventures
Princeton, New Jersey

Office "bay window"

The upper three floors of an existing nineteenth century office building in Princeton were renovated for a capital investment firm. The clients required separate offices for the three principal partners with provision for two future junior partners. All were to share centralized secretarial services and a conference room which was intended to be the most private space.

Major sections of the structure between the second floor and the roof were removed and an independent system of columns and beams was erected within the resulting volume. The open plan arrangement placed within this spatial context allows privacy where required without disrupting an overall reading of the open space. The zones of activity are distributed hierarchically along the main axis; the conference room is placed at the head of the axis on the street edge.

A two-story mural gives visual extension to the space and unites the two floors of open offices adjacent to it. References to the landscape both in this mural and in the polychromed elements throughout the offices provide a metaphorical dimension to the scheme, which complements the openness of the plan and suggests that a continuity exists between the interior spaces of the new office and the outdoor roof terrace beyond.

Professional Office, Gunwyn Ventures

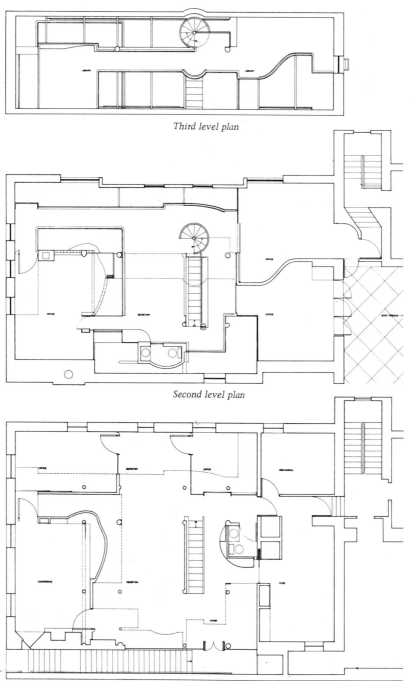

Third level plan

Second level plan

First level plan

Existing building

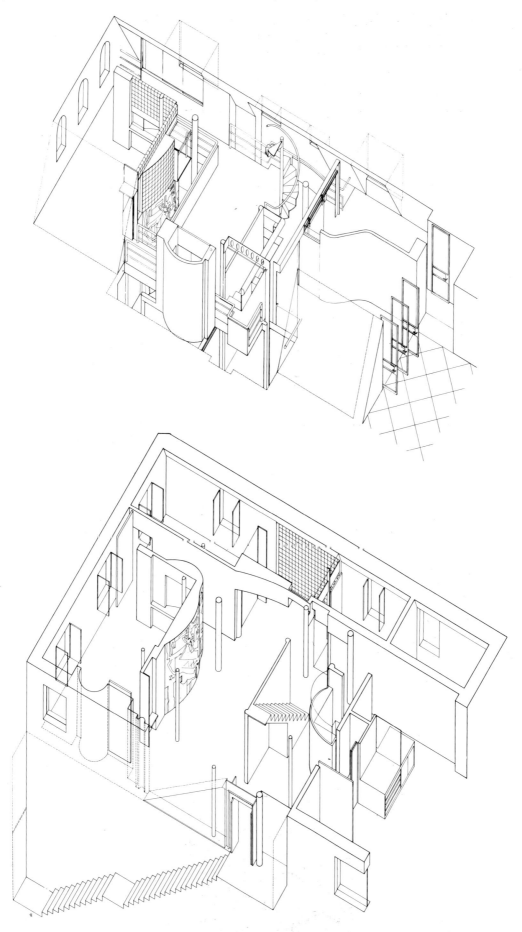

First and second level axonometrics

Partner's office door

Stair to third level

Third level

Second level secretarial space

View of stair from second floor

View of upper levels from entrance

Second level secretarial space

1971 and 1973

Alexander House
Princeton, New Jersey

Oblique view of garden facade

This addition to a 1930's colonial-style house includes a kitchen, breakfast room, potting area, desk, and sitting room within one 900 square foot space on the ground floor.

The original house, like many of neoclassical descent, has a quadripartite plan with a central entrance hall. The addition, similar in size to one quadrant of the original house, has its own four-part organization and its own center. As one moves from dining room to kitchen to breakfast room to garden along the new central axis, the spaces become more open and filled with light. This is accomplished by the use of glass block, clerestory glazing and an open frame at the outer edge. The curving glass block wall of the breakfast room both allows the rather free disposition of activity spaces relative to the overall organization of the grid inside and, because of its picturesque quality, is sympathetic to the nature of the garden beyond.

An open trellis-like frame across the back of the house extends the garden facade and partially encloses an existing porch. Above the frame, a steel "window" sculpture refers to the master bedroom window on the main house behind it. The "window" is aligned with the central axis of the house and swung outward like an open casement, implying the opening of the bedroom to the view of the garden beyond.

A separate addition on the second floor includes a guest room and a library whose mural, placed on an existing windowless wall facing the garden, visually extends the interior space. As the existing windows of the library provide an actual view of the outdoors, the mural, in balance, creates a metaphoric landscape of its own.

Breakfast room soffit

Porch frame detail

Breakfast room interior

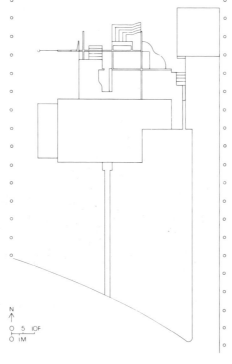

N
↑
0 5 10F
0 1M

Site plan

Oblique view of garden facade

Alexander House

Garden facade

Breakfast room

Second floor library with mural

Bay window and desk

View of terrace from breakfast room

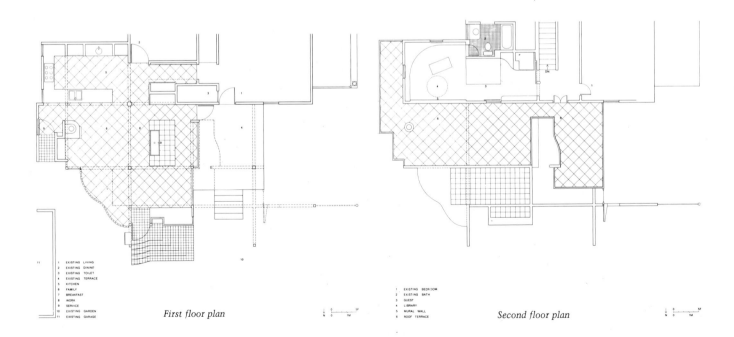

1   EXISTING LIVING
2   EXISTING DINING
3   EXISTING TOILET
4   EXISTING TERRACE
5   KITCHEN
6   FAMILY
7   BREAKFAST
8   WORK
9   SERVICE
10   EXISTING GARDEN
11   EXISTING GARAGE

First floor plan

1   EXISTING BEDROOM
2   EXISTING BATH
3   GUEST
4   LIBRARY
5   MURAL WALL
6   ROOF TERRACE

Second floor plan

Family room

Breakfast room interior

Sculpture "Open Window"

1974

Wageman House
Princeton, New Jersey

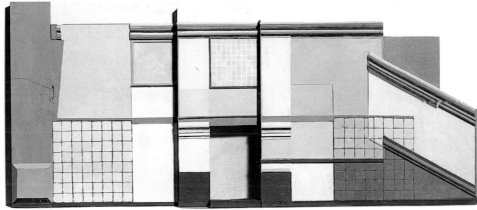

Facade study model

In this project, the garage of an existing house is converted into a studio on the ground floor and a master bedroom and bath above. A new street facade extends across the front, enclosing a private garden for the studio between the original house and the new wall. This new facade attempts to organize the disparate volumes of the two-story addition and the existing one-story house and provides a new entrance in the area between garage and house. The depth of the forecourt is indicated on the facade by the ground-like dark green panel. Above this panel, the molding set at an angle is parallel with the cornice of the original house, suggesting that the new facade be read as garden wall enclosure. This molding, together with the panels of diminishing size, sets up a perspective drive toward the entrance. The symmetrical location of the gridded panels further emphasizes the "center". In the earlier scheme, the suggestion of a split pediment is used to call attention to the importance of the entrance.

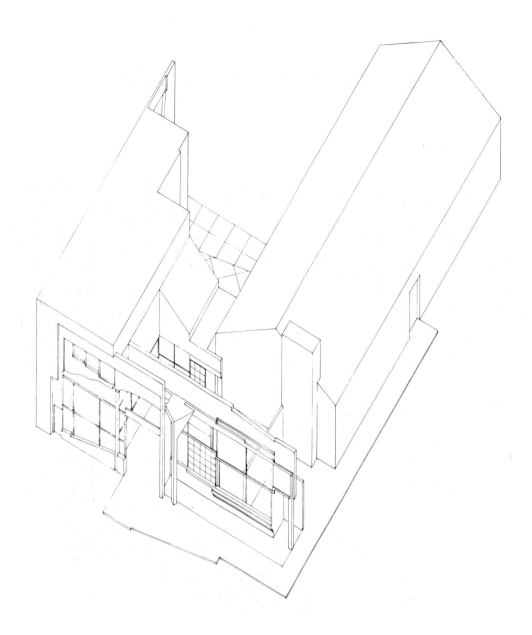

Model of preliminary scheme

1975

Housing for the Elderly
Competition
Trenton, New Jersey

West view of model

The program for this competition, sponsored by the New Jersey Society of Architects, included 120 one-bedroom apartments to be rented to the elderly, as well as communal social spaces, outdoor recreation spaces, and short- and long-term parking. In the building, communal spaces are located on the ground floor near the entrance to maximize social contact and to maintain the privacy of the individual dwellings above.

The specified density of site coverage required the building to be larger than the three- and four-story frame dwellings in the surrounding neighborhood. The institutional image often associated with a high rise block is diminished here by reducing the scale of the facades and by making an irregular curve of the primary entrance facade. The grouping of the windows into larger units by the exterior frame masks the thirteen story bulk of the building and, combined with the use of tile on the surface, develops a scalar relationship with the surrounding neighborhood. The housing is oriented to the park-like setting of the area and its major parking is placed off the site on a nearby street. The building is thus not separated from its surroundings and generous light and a good view are assured for each unit. The free-form curve of the facade establishes a relationship with the landscape and elaborates the zone of transition from landscape to building.

Lobby interior

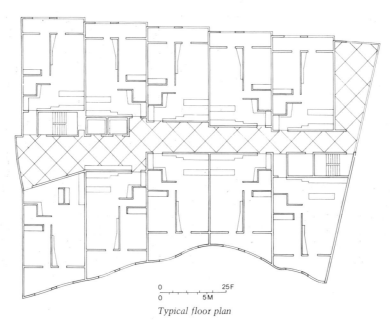

0   25F
0   5M

Typical floor plan

Site plan

1974

Claghorn House
Princeton, New Jersey

View from the northeast

The Claghorn House, an 1890's white clapboard Queen Anne style building, is located on a half-acre lot in Princeton. The addition, which includes a kitchen, breakfast room, bar, china pantry, garden room and porch, links the house to its rear garden. Each of these functional areas is given a different space, defined by explicit structural elements such as columns, beams, and screens. The spaces are organized in layers that progress from enclosed to more open as one moves toward the garden. On the kitchen side of the addition, there is a china pantry and bar which is used as a sitting area, a cooking area, and a breakfast table which is oriented toward the garden through a large window. On the porch side, the garden room, a transitional space between the garden and the house, is separated from the dining room by segments of the original wall of the main house. The garden room has a glass wall leading onto the porch. A dropped ceiling over the garden room and the diagonal tile on the dining room floor provide perspectival connection with the kitchen.

Over the porch, a cruciform post and beam construction divides the space into quadrants and forms a gate or frame over the porch stairs. The crossing suggests enclosure by making a window-like gesture to the sky; the underside of the beam crossing is painted blue to reinforce that reference. The deck is also linked conceptually to the ground by the use of plinth-like planters alongside the stairs.

The addition is related visually to the original house by the use of direct references to its classical and neoclassical antecedents. These references, often quite literal, take the form of traditional devices like latticework, suggestive of sun-filled garden structures, broken pediments symbolizing man's occupation of the center, and string coursing alluding to one's assumption of the floor as transposed ground plane. These are reinterpreted here to reinforce their symbolic and actual roles or meanings as elements of architecture. The use of color refers to the antecedents of the older house and also to nature, particularly to the surrounding garden.

Porch detail

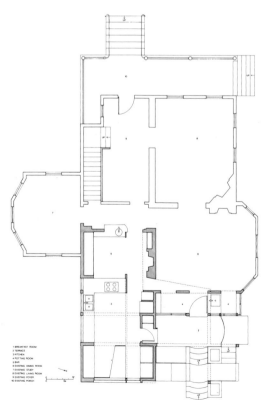

1 BREAKFAST ROOM
2 TERRACE
3 KITCHEN
4 POTTING ROOM
5 BAR
6 EXISTING DINING ROOM
7 EXISTING STUDY
8 EXISTING LIVING ROOM
9 EXISTING FOYER
10 EXISTING PORCH

Plan of original house and addition

North elevation

East elevation

Kitchen

Dining room wall

Window detail

Stair detail

Terrace detail

View of terrace from the north

1975

The Newark Museum
Carriage House Renovation
Newark, New Jersey

View of entrance from the garden

The program for the Newark Museum Carriage House renovation calls for its conversion to a museum for modern painting and sculpture. The Victorian building, constructed in the 1890's, is separated from the main museum complex by an open space to be developed into a sculpture garden and an amphitheater for noontime concerts. A gesture of enclosure is created by the form of the amphitheater and the lyric quality of the hedge wall bounding the garden. The hedge is extended metaphorically into the building on an axis which organizes the exhibits inside according to their requirements for natural light. The artifacts suggested to be exhibited outdoors vary from landscape frames or gates such as those found in the sculpture of Anthony Caro, to modern figural sculpture such as Picasso's "Bathers". These establish formal and ritual themes in the composition both by their placement in the landscape and by their allegorical or metaphorical associations.

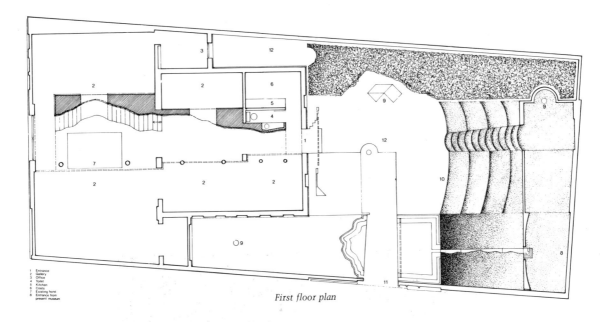

1 Entrance
2 Gallery
3 Office
4 Toilet
5 Kitchen
6 Coats
7 Existing hoist
8 Entrance from
  present museum

First floor plan

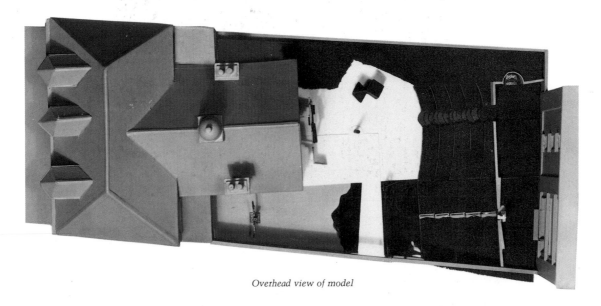

Overhead view of model

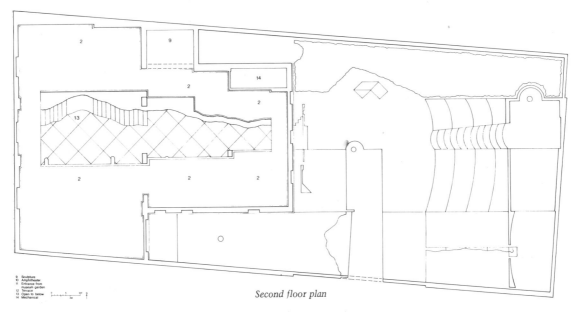

9 Sculpture
10 Amphitheater
11 Entrance from
   museum garden
12 Terrace
13 Open to below
14 Mechanical

Second floor plan

1976

Crooks House
Fort Wayne, Indiana

Northwest facade study

The site for the Crooks House is a three quarter acre lot in a wooded suburban subdivision in the midst of a series of development houses. The typical suburban solution to the problem of privacy, as evident in the surrounding houses, is to locate the building as an isolated object in the approximate center of the site, thereby leaving the landscape as residue. While privacy is accomplished by isolation in the surrounding tract houses, the Crooks House derives its privacy by treating the formal gestures as fragments of a larger organization, thereby setting up a dependence of object and landscape. Rather than a single center, a succession of centers is produced both in the building and in the landscape. These centers are linked and can be understood as a spatial continuum. While the Crooks House is very small, providing accommodation for a family of two adults and one child, it extends its sphere of influence by the fragmentation of both building and landscape. In this way, the residual character of the adjoining sites is diminished and a spatial continuity which provides for necessary levels of public and private domain is established.

Facing the street are the kitchen and garage walls, connected by a screen wall with an opening for the driveway. The drive ends in a court formed by the house, garage, and garden. From the court, one enters the house on an axis of light provided by three skylights within a double-height volume crossed by bridges at an upper level. On the left, past a glass block partition, is the living room which receives most of its natural light from a large skylight above the fireplace. On the back side of the fireplace is the sitting room which, like the living room, has windows only in the wall facing the garden. The wall is pulled out at an angle from the house's volume. Upstairs, a terrace off the master bedroom occupies this space between the wall and the cubiform volume of the house. On the second floor, there are two bedrooms and a study which can be converted into a third bedroom in the future.

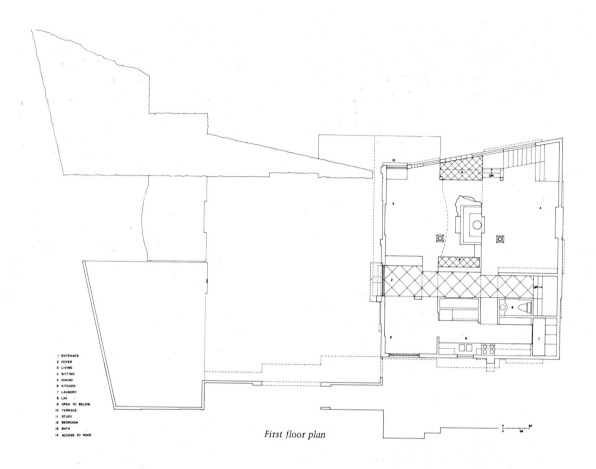

1 ENTRANCE
2 FOYER
3 LIVING
4 SITTING
5 DINING
6 KITCHEN
7 LAUNDRY
8 LAV
9 OPEN TO BELOW
10 TERRACE
11 STUDY
12 BEDROOM
13 BATH
14 ACCESS TO ROOF

First floor plan

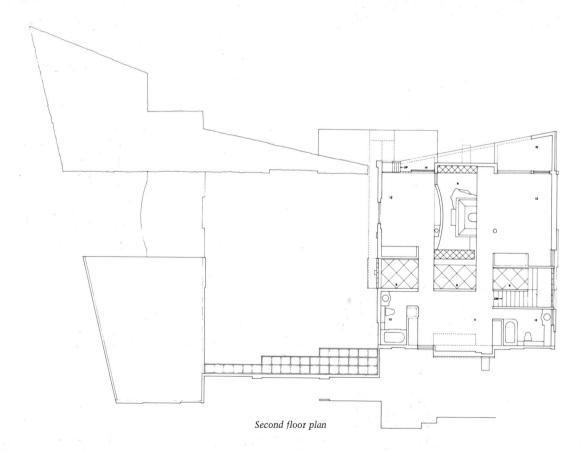

Second floor plan

Overhead view of model

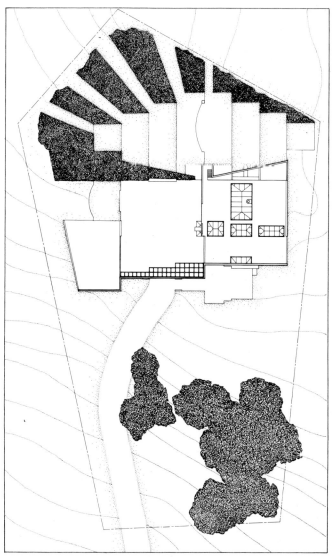

Site plan

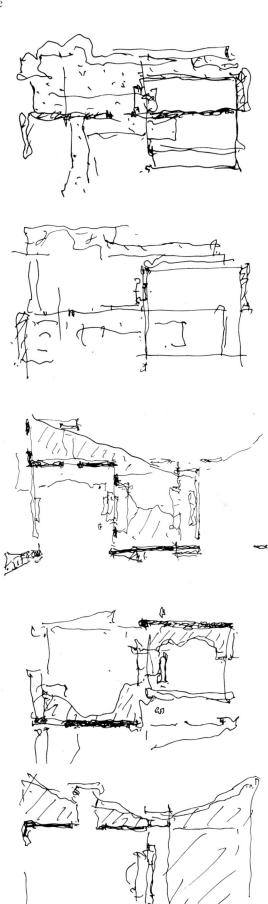

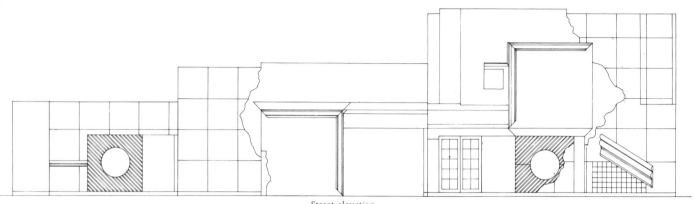

Street elevation

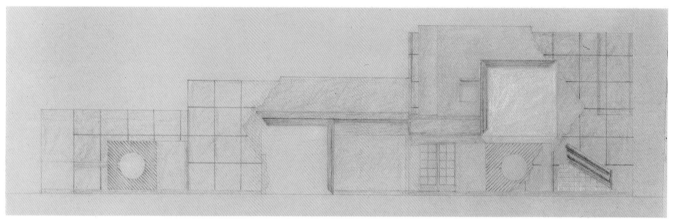

Street elevation

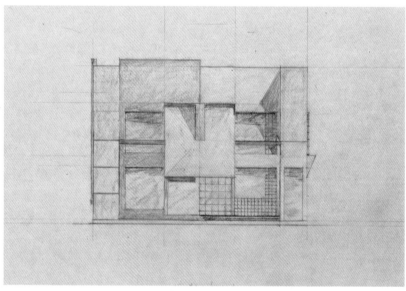

Garden elevation study

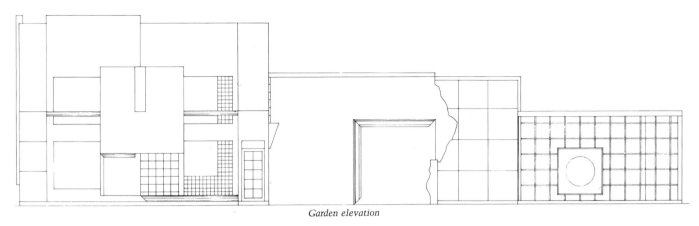

Garden elevation

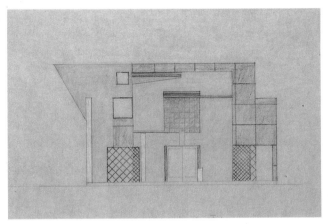

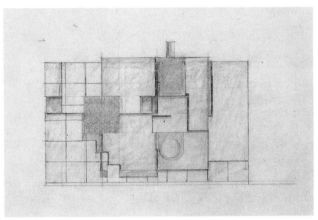

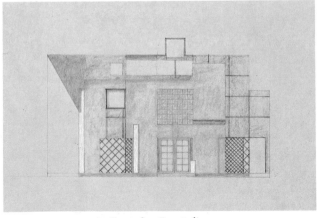

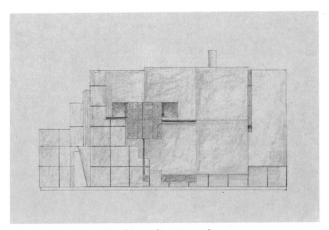

Court elevation studies

Northwest elevation studies

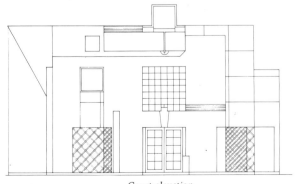

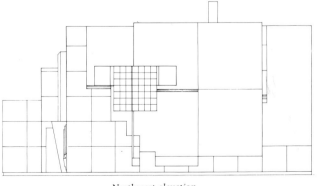

Court elevation

Northwest elevation

View of model from the street

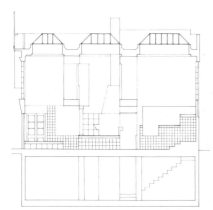

Section through entrance and hall

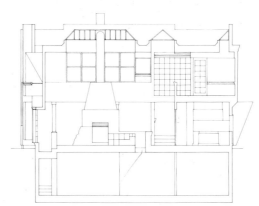

Section through living and kitchen

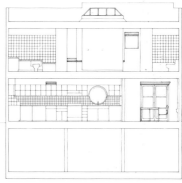

Section through dining and kitchen

South view of model

Fireplace

1976

Schulman House
Princeton, New Jersey

Street facade

In this project, a new living room and garden wall have been added to a two-story suburban house. The three elements of the composition are discrete in plan but are linked serially in the street elevation by their progressively decreasing size and the repetition of similar formal elements. As each segment steps forward in plan, the dimensions of the lapped siding increase in the elevation, thereby setting up a forced perspective which accentuates the new entry in the street facade. On the garden side, a new center is made by a screened porch which connects the living room addition with a former garage, now used for storage. The center is reinforced by the symmetrical relationship of the fenetration of the living room wall and the gridded frame applied to the garage wall.

The addition has been polychromed to reflect its relation to the garden or landscape. An attempt was made to root the building in the ground by placing the representation of the garden, dark green, at the base of the facade. Next, a terra cotta belt coursing has been used to register the idea of the raised ground plane or ground floor within the house. The green facade is continued above to suggest the addition as a garden room but is given a lighter value as if washed by light. The composition is capped by a blue cornice with a second minor belting of terra cotta, suggesting the juxtaposition to the soffit or sky.

Schulman House

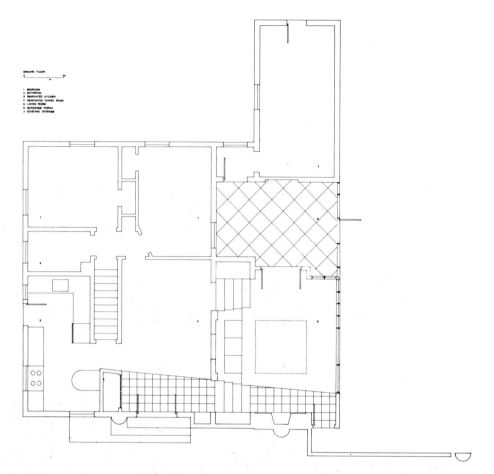

GROUND FLOOR

1 BEDROOM
2 BATHROOM
3 RENOVATED KITCHEN
4 RENOVATED DINING ROOM
5 LIVING ROOM
6 SCREENED PORCH
7 EXISTING STORAGE

Plan of original house and addition

Preliminary studies

Street elevation

View of original house from the street

View of original house from the garden

Garden elevation

Garden facade

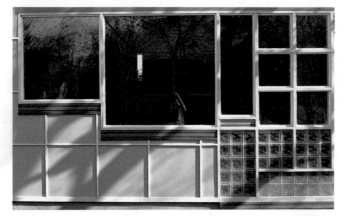 

View of living room from dining room

Living room

View of fireplace wall from dining room

Oblique view of street facade

1977

Warehouse Conversion
Graves House
Princeton, New Jersey

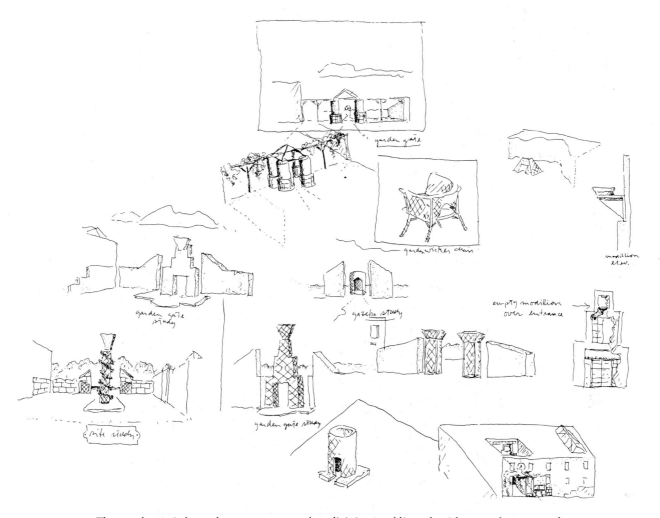

garden gate

garden wicker chair

modillion elev.

garden gate study

gazebo study

empty modillion over entrance

(site study)

garden gate study

The warehouse is located on a quarter-acre lot adjoining a public park with access from an established residential street. The building was built in 1926 of hollow clay tile surfaced with brick and stucco. It is a two-story L-shaped structure, which, in its original state, was divided into small storage cells along a central corridor in each wing. The renovation provides living accommodations for a family of two adults and four children.

An attempt was made in the design to comment on the ambiance of the existing structure which was built in a typical Tuscan vernacular manner by Italian masons who were then employed in the construction of Princeton University. The existing openings (truck docks) were used as the primary entrances to the building in an effort to preserve the surface value of the facades. To identify the primary entrance and to gain light in the depth of the building without greatly altering the exterior walls, a courtyard excision was made into the structure. Elements of the new construction were thus established inside the body of the building. The overall simplicity of the existing interior and exterior surfaces was left intact; however, the new surfaces have been elaborated with figural elements in order to allow a closer identification with classical and anthropomorphic sources.

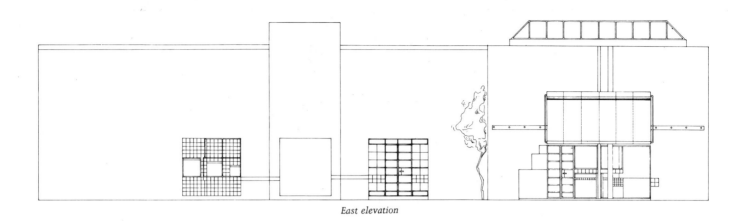

East elevation

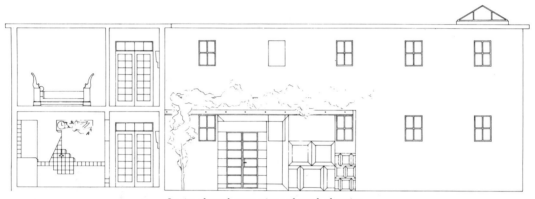

Section through west wing and south elevation

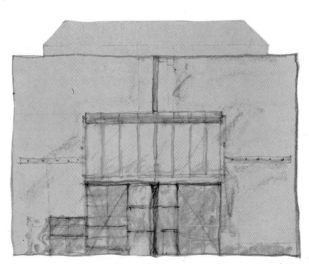

East elevation study

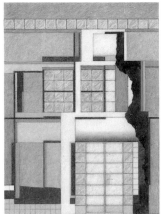

Courtyard entrance triptych

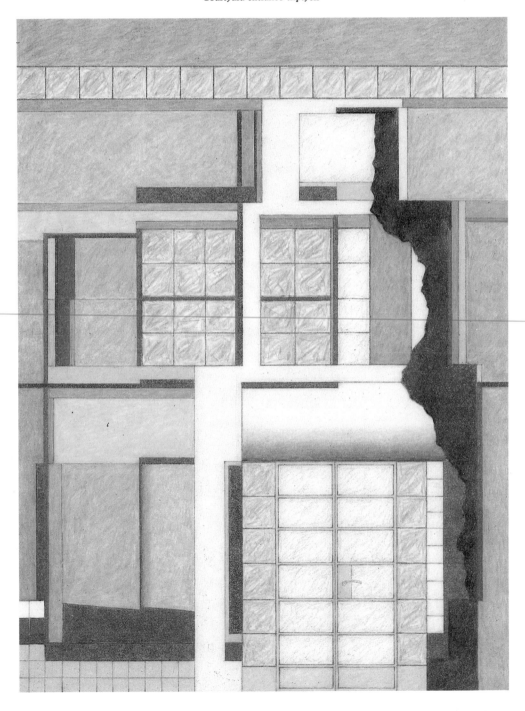

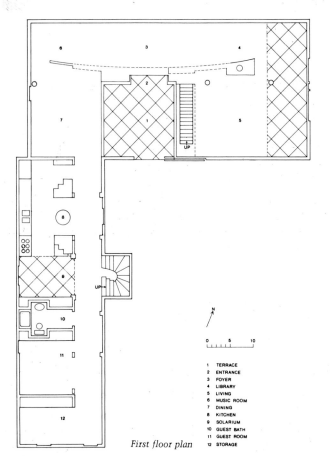

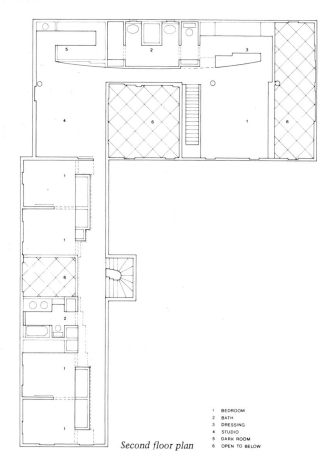

First floor plan

1 TERRACE
2 ENTRANCE
3 FOYER
4 LIBRARY
5 LIVING
6 MUSIC ROOM
7 DINING
8 KITCHEN
9 SOLARIUM
10 GUEST BATH
11 GUEST ROOM
12 STORAGE

Second floor plan

1 BEDROOM
2 BATH
3 DRESSING
4 STUDIO
5 DARK ROOM
6 OPEN TO BELOW

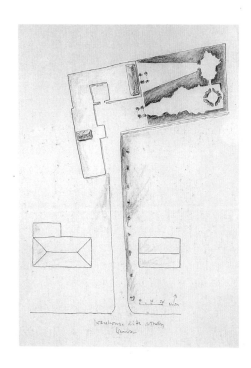

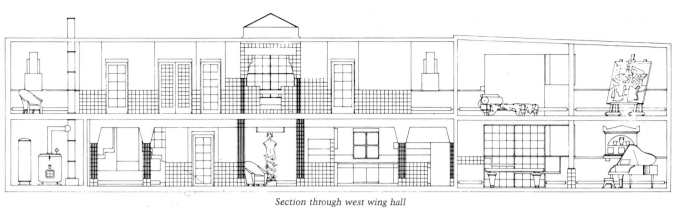

Section through west wing hall

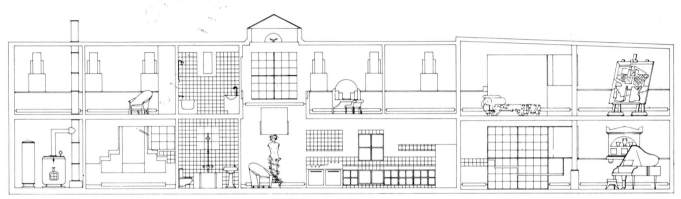

Section through west wing

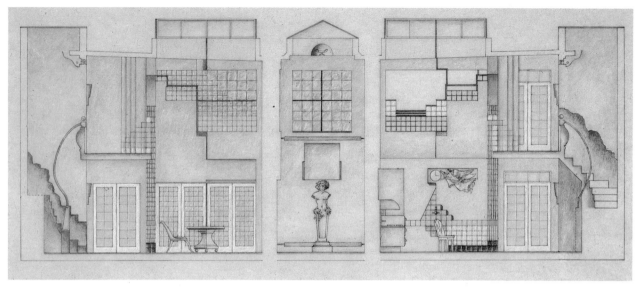

Solarium

Section through west wing hall

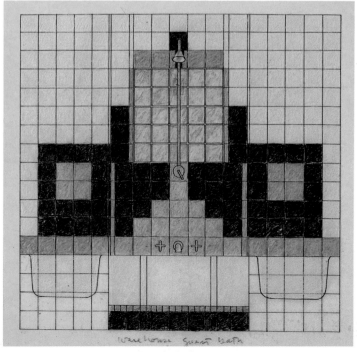

Guest bath elevation

Second floor bathroom

Guest bath

Solarium

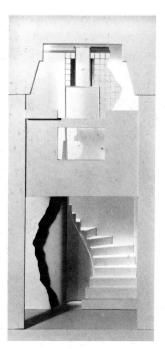

West wing stair model

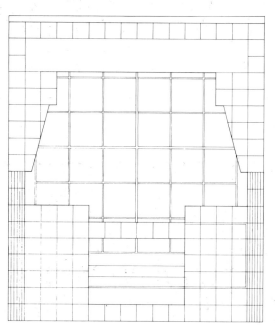
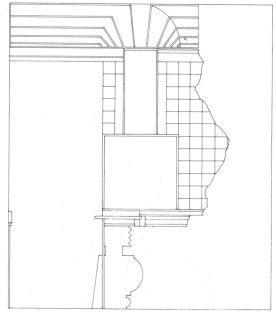

Stair landing elevations

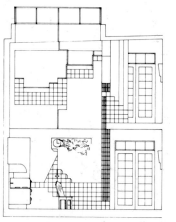
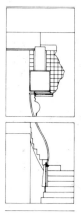
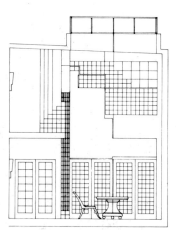

Solarium

Kitchen entrance

View of courtyard from the south

1977

"Artists' Postcards"

Postcard "Pre and Post Card"

A number of artists were asked to re-explore the characteristics of postcard art for a travelling exhibition and a limited edition of postcards. This example is an assemblage which uses both the idea of message and the nostalgia of familiar postcard images.

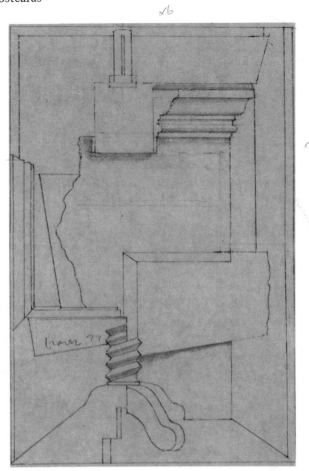

1977

Chem-Fleur Factory Addition and Renovation
Newark, New Jersey

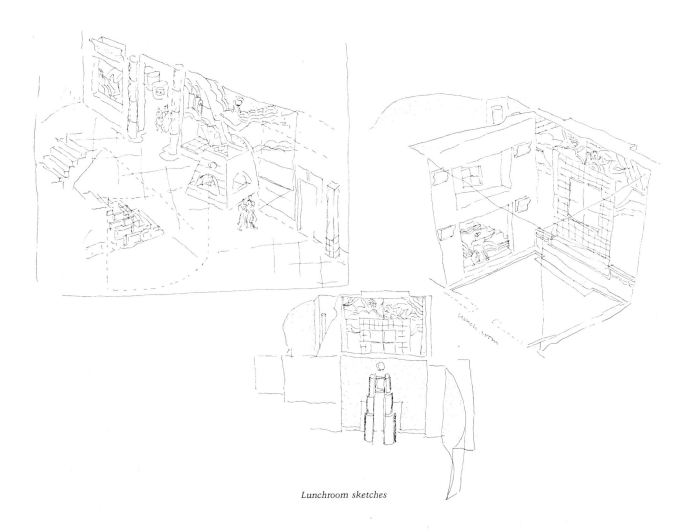

Lunchroom sketches

The client, a Newark-based research and processing company, required that new employee facilities, administrative offices, and a warehouse be added to the existing plant. Also, laboratory space in the plant was to be renovated.

The three parts of the program—offices, warehouse, and factory—remain distinct elements of the overall organization of the project. They are located on the site according to both their internal relationships and their differing needs for access from the street. The central circulation spine in the original building is extended through the addition, binding the three parts of the plan. This axis is terminated in the common room of the office building, in keeping with the primacy of this space in the internal organization of the factory. The street entrance to the office building leads through a foyer to the reception area which, with the common room, forms a system of interlocking centers, thereby connecting the two principal axes.

The inter-relationship of the three elements of the plan is also reflected in the west facade, where the old and new are superimposed. The juncture of the existing laboratory building and the warehouse addition is further articulated volumetrically by a skylit void between them. The north facade of the office building, by the organization and size of the windows, differentiates the collective or shared spaces such as the lunchroom and common room on one side from the individual, repetitive offices on the other.

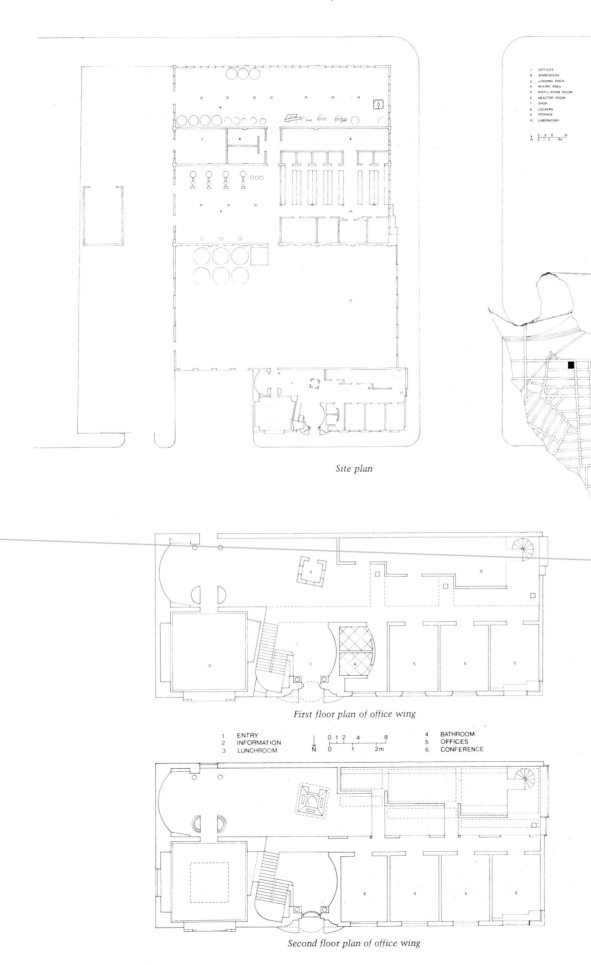

Site plan

First floor plan of office wing

1	ENTRY	4	BATHROOM
2	INFORMATION	5	OFFICES
3	LUNCHROOM	6	CONFERENCE

Second floor plan of office wing

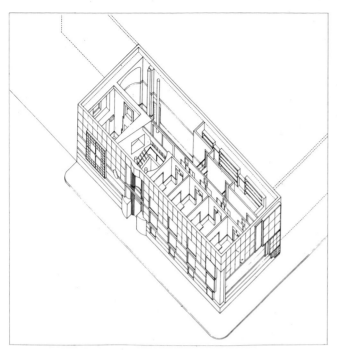

Office building axonometric

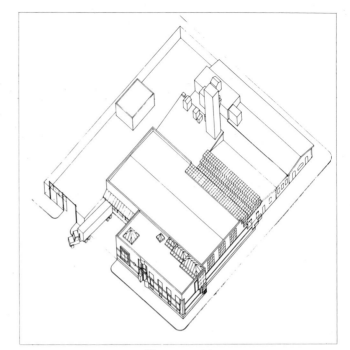

Site axonometric

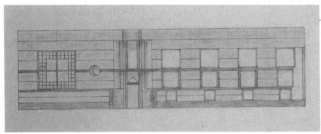

Entrance elevation

West elevation of the office building and factory complex

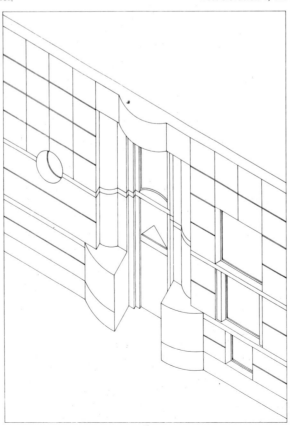

Entrance

Fargo–Moorhead Cultural Center Bridge
Fargo, North Dakota and Moorhead, Minnesota

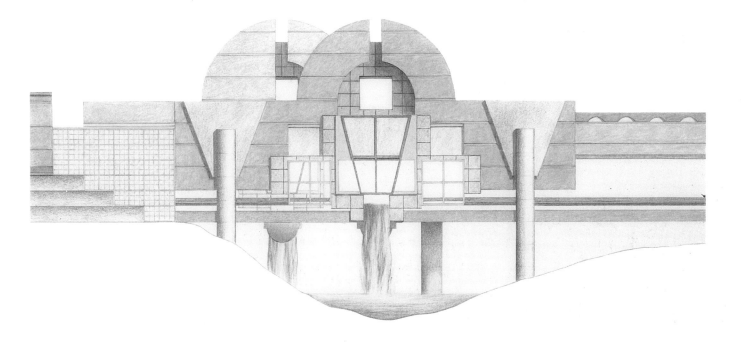

Fargo and Moorhead are twin cities in the adjacent states of North Dakota and Minnesota, separated by the Red River of the North. In conjunction with the replacement of a vehicular bridge, a cultural center is planned which would physically and symbolically link the two communities. An art museum spans the bridge and connects a concert hall and public radio and television stations on one side with a history museum on the other.

The concert hall and radio and television station complex incorporates the Case Building, an existing three-story structure, and uses its key position on the site as a significant element in the composition. This building, which is to be remodelled, will accommodate radio and television and provide support spaces for the concert hall. The double entry to this complex was required because of local traffic conditions and the location of public parking facilities. The concert hall is located between these two portals and a common lobby, also to be used for exhibitions, gives access to the art museum on the bridge.

A common lobby is also developed between the history and art museums which will share a lecture hall and temporary exhibition space as well. Exhibitions are arranged in a loop around the central lecture hall and extend out into the landscape along the banks of the river. The building's greenhouse-like enclosure on the river side and the picturesque quality of its configuration reinforce the connection to the outside and attempt to draw a parallel between the artifacts exhibited and their derivation from the land.

The art museum is located on the north side of the bridge above the pedestrian and vehicular roadways. The public corridor through the building is developed as a linear gallery. On the south side of the bridge, a large outdoor porch overlooks the river and the amphitheater outside the concert hall.

In the composition, a vertical unity is attempted by employing the river itself as the basement story, the vehicular access and the first level bridge as *piano nobile*, and the art museum above the bridge as attic. The horizontal linking members, which are covered aerial walkways connecting the three cultural facilities, are seen as the cornice line of a continuous building, allowing for compositional completeness.

In its facades, the bridge employs enlarged symbolic elements of architecture such as keystones, which have been made void as windows, bringing together the two cities by providing a focus on the river and establishing it as center. The voided keystone is also seen as a scupper which collects the sky and replenishes the river below through a waterfall which issues from its base. The water is pumped from the river by a windmill which is part of the history museum and reflects the agrarian base of the communities. In this way, the individual elements of the composition are seen as parts of a larger narrative.

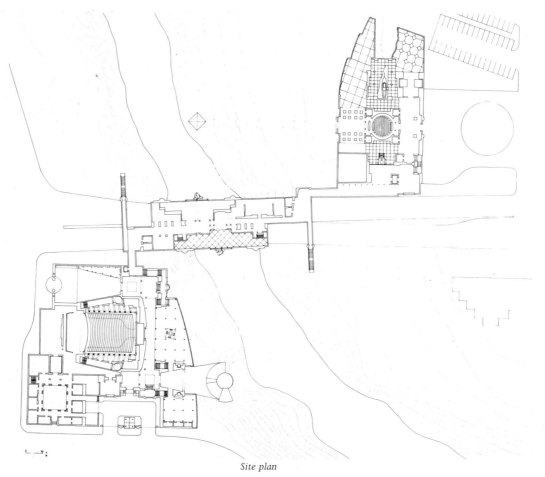

Site plan

Southeast view of the site model

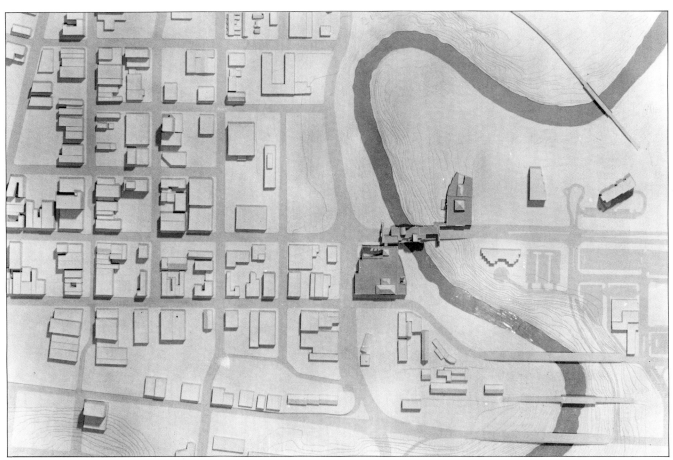

Overhead view of site model

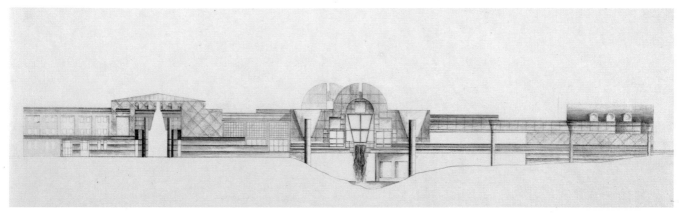

Preliminary south elevation

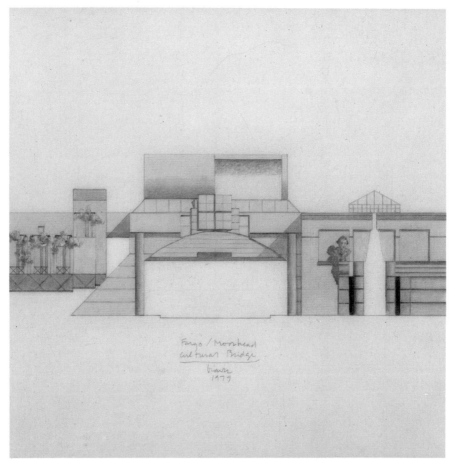

West elevation

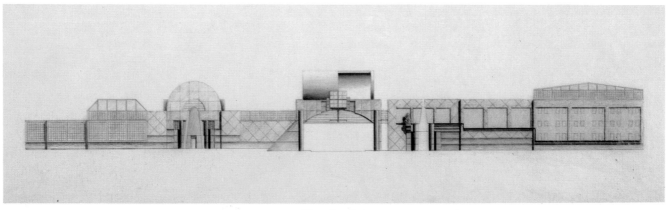

West elevation

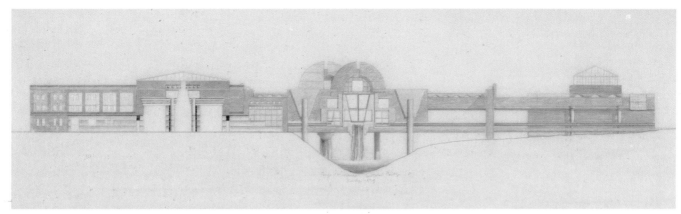

South elevation

South elevation

South view of model

West view of model

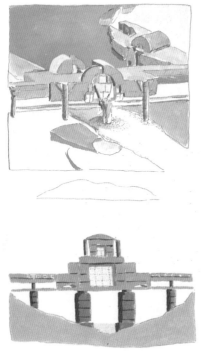
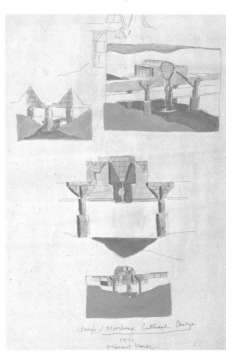

Bridge studies

1977

Plocek House
Warren, New Jersey

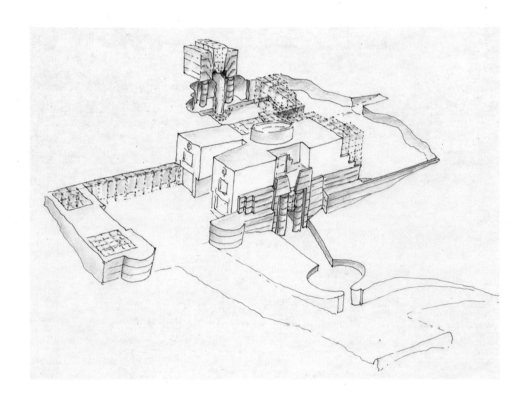

The Plocek House is situated on a wooded hillside in Warren, New Jersey. The three stories of the house are expressed in the street facade whose articulation recalls the classical tripartite division of basement, *piano nobile*, and attic. One enters the house through this facade at the lower level and also through the east facade at the main level, adjacent to the parking court. The intersection of these two entry axes is marked by a stair column with its base at the lower entry level, its shaft on the main living level, and its capital in the upper story providing light from above.

In the composition, house and landscape are made formally interdependent. Along the primary entrance axis, a gate relating to the basement story is pulled away from the front facade while the study pavilion in the garden is seen as the keystone removed from the mass of the upper portion of the house. The relationship of the house to the site is clarified by the understanding that these elements have been displaced and are located along the processional axis of the house. Furthermore, a series of stepped walls, one of which engages the study pavilion, forms the outer edge of the rear garden, whose figure is completed by the garden facade of the house itself. As the house can now be seen as a fragment within this total organization of building and landscape, the thematic dialogue between the two is both understood and enriched.

119

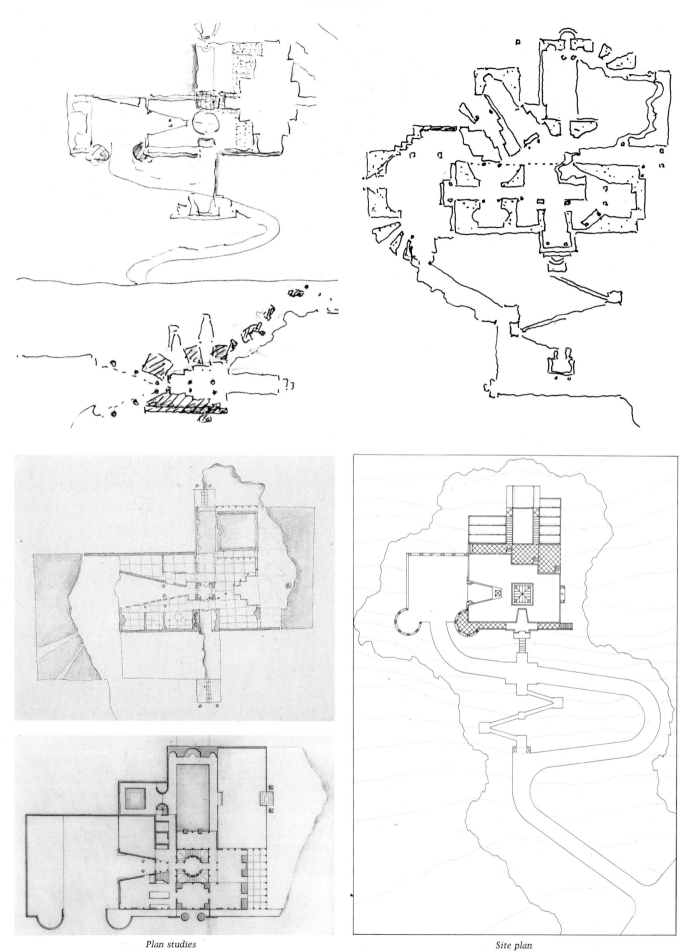

Plan studies

Site plan

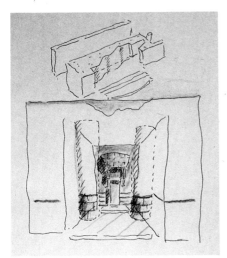

Court entrance study

Referential sketch; Lutyens gate house

Entrance study

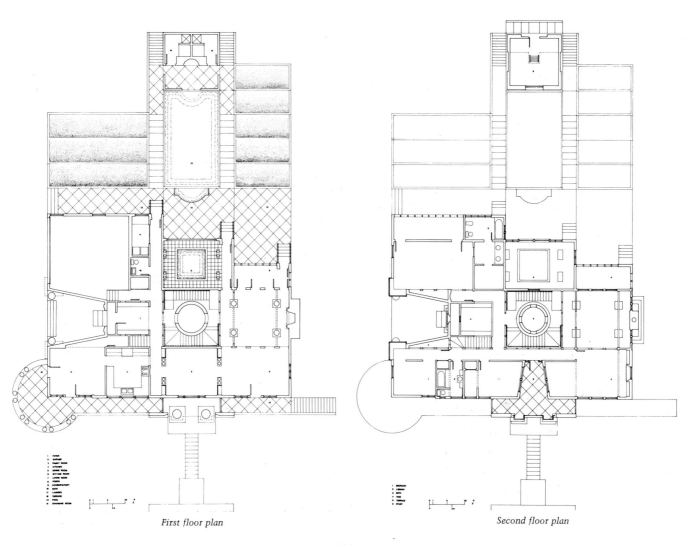

First floor plan

Second floor plan

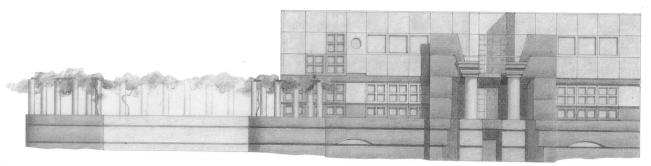

Street elevation

Model view of the street facade

Plocek House

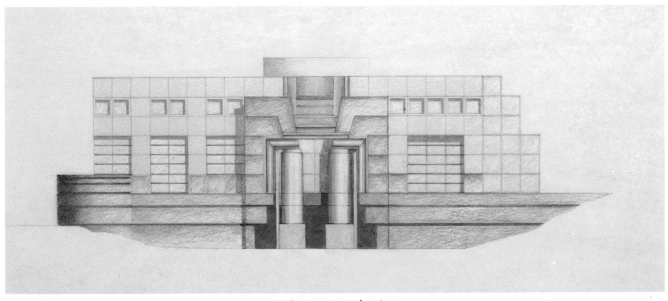

Preliminary street elevation

Preliminary garden elevation

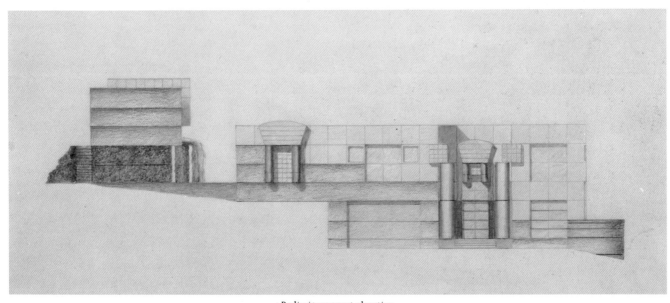

Preliminary court elevation

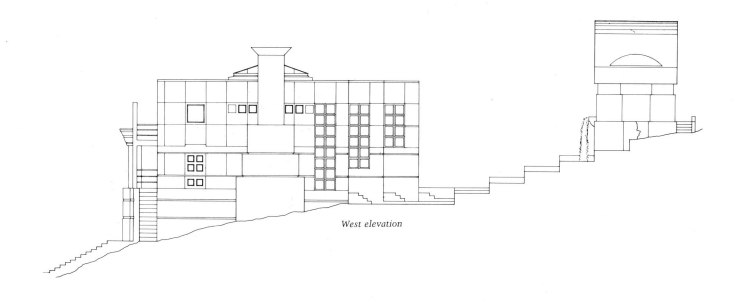

West elevation

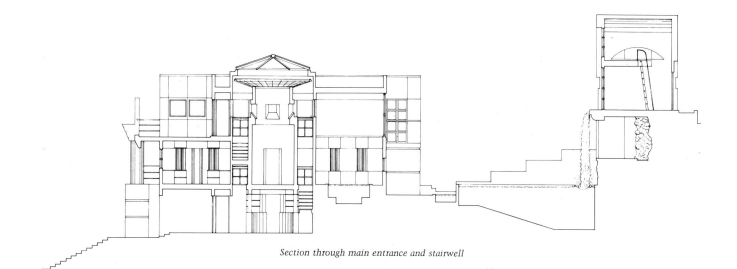

Section through main entrance and stairwell

Building under construction

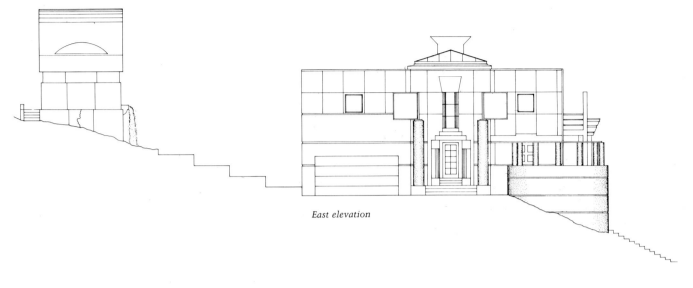

East elevation

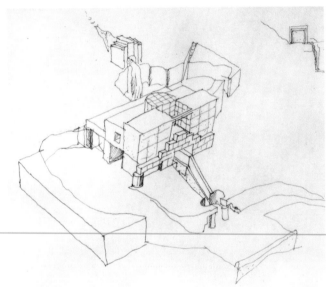

Axonometric study

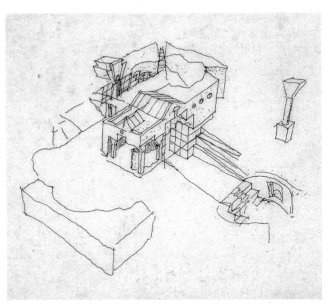

Axonometric study

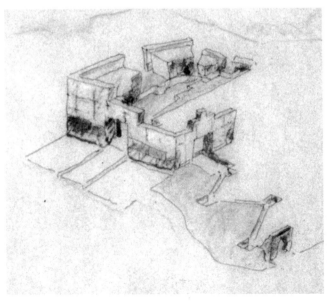

Axonometric study

Axonometric study

Model view of the street facade and poolhouse

Model view of the court facade

Model view of the garden facade

Construction photograph, view from the street

Garden facade under construction

Oblique view of garden facade under construction

Main entrance under construction

1978

"Roma Interrotta" Exhibition
Rome, Italy

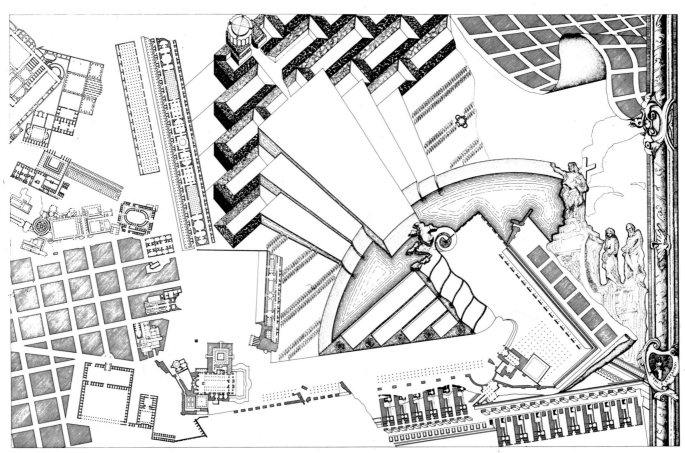

Final scheme for the Porta Maggiore section

"Roma Interrotta," an exhibition sponsored by the Italian Ministry of Transportation, is based on the map of Rome made by Giambattista Nolli in 1748. This map was divided into twelve sections to facilitate the printing of the original plates. For the exhibition, twelve internationally known architects were each assigned a section and asked to use it as a base for "interventions." The title of the exhibition, "Roma Interrotta," or "Rome Interrupted," signifies the intention of making urban assumptions from Nolli's base plan. No requirements for particular activities were given, so the participants could specify those which they deemed appropriate for their sector.

In this scheme for the Porta Maggiore section of Rome, figurative fragments, such as the keystone garden, have been used in an attempt to employ elements of an architectural language not only in their orthodox locations, but also for their potential as symbolic anologies. The keystone garden is surrounded by an assemblage of Roman buildings and urban types which, together with the newly designed elements and reinstated ancient fragments from the site, incorporate housing, commercial, and cultural activities.

128

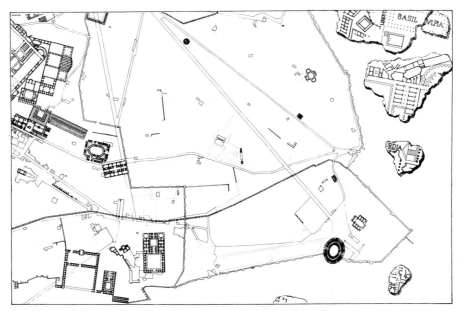

Porta Maggiore section of ancient Rome

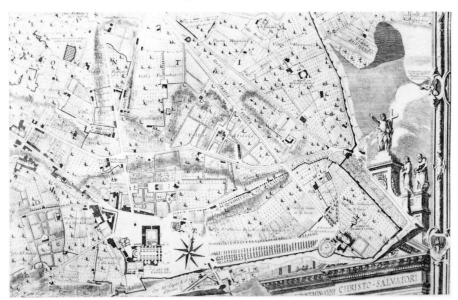

Porta Maggiore section of the Nolli map of Rome

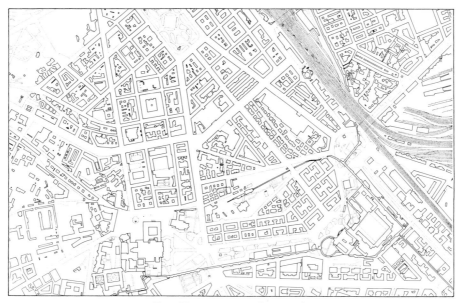

Porta Maggiore section of Rome today

Cover design for the Roma Interrota issue of Architectural Design

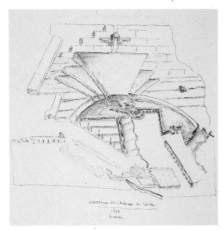

Study sketch for the "Keystone Garden" *Passegiata a Minerva Medica sketch* *Study sketch for "Fragmentary Housing"*

1977

Private Dance Studio
Princeton, New Jersey

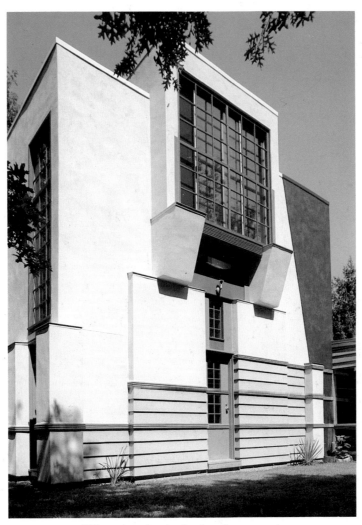

Oblique view of garden facade under construction

The addition to this one-story suburban house built in the 1950's includes, on the first floor, a private dance studio for the client who is a choreographer, and on the second floor, a master bedroom and study. The existing building, with its butterfly roof and cedar siding, is drawn into the composition. The cedar siding is extended across the addition, forming a base for the "lighter" building above. The upper, stuccoed portion of the building is to be latticed, as if it were a garden gazebo. The centralizing element of the main garden facade, which includes a lower entry door between paired columns that support an oversized "dormer" window, is an attempt to make the addition understandable as a pavilion or object in the garden. This idea of separation can be read simultaneously with the sense of continuity with the existing context achieved through the use of cedar siding at the lower level.

Preliminary studies

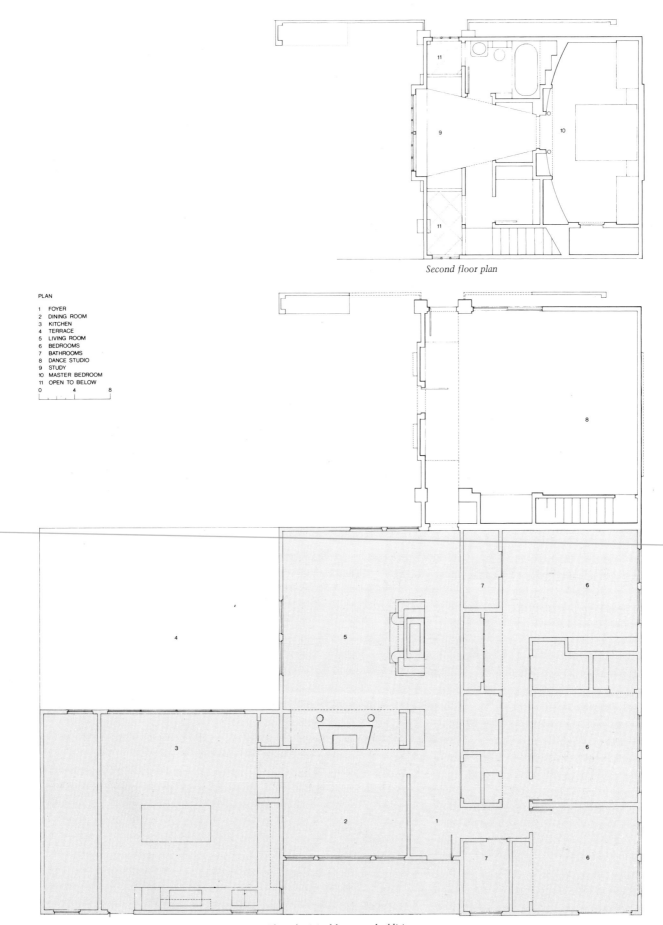

Second floor plan

PLAN

1 FOYER
2 DINING ROOM
3 KITCHEN
4 TERRACE
5 LIVING ROOM
6 BEDROOMS
7 BATHROOMS
8 DANCE STUDIO
9 STUDY
10 MASTER BEDROOM
11 OPEN TO BELOW

0   4   8

Plan of original house and addition

Preliminary south elevation

Preliminary south elevation

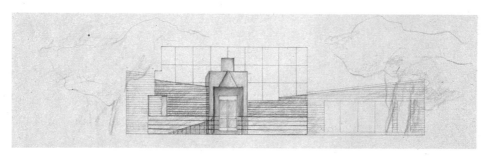

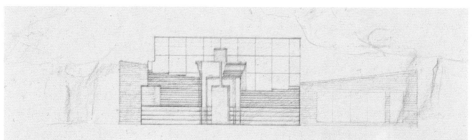

Preliminary west elevations

South elevation

North elevation

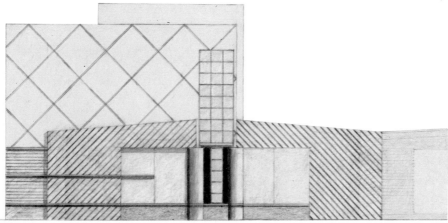

West elevation

Garden facade under construction

Fireplace

1978

Private Residence
Green Brook, New Jersey

The house is located in a clearing of a densely wooded site which slopes steeply to the back and side, offering a distant but dramatic view of New York City. The program for this house for two adults may be considered conventional, in that it includes living spaces, dining room, kitchen, master bedroom, and guest room, but it is particularized in this case by the need to accommodate the client's collection of foreign automobiles. The inclusion of numerous garages thus becomes a primary factor in the organization of the site. A wing of garages provides enclosure on one side of the entrance forecourt, and, in concert with a small free-standing garage pavilion, makes a gate on the street.

A typical French courtyard scheme, which would have two parallel side walls flanking a centrally disposed house, is varied here to describe the second major site influence, a large outdoor pool. The automobile forecourt, partially defined by buildings, is completed by the landscape, while the "missing" wing of the typical French courtyard model is displaced to the garden to enclose the pool. The skewed orientation of the second wing, along with the echelon of the garden facade itself, encourages the oblique view of Manhattan beyond.

Private Residence

Axonometric study

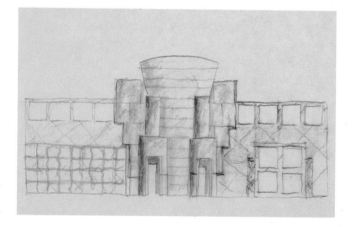

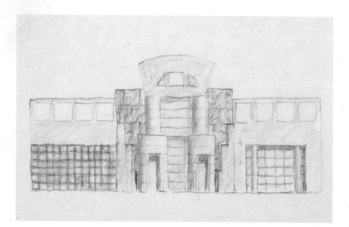

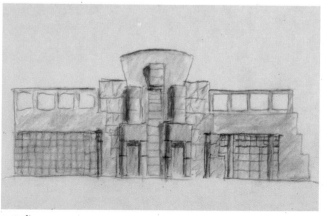

Garden elevation studies

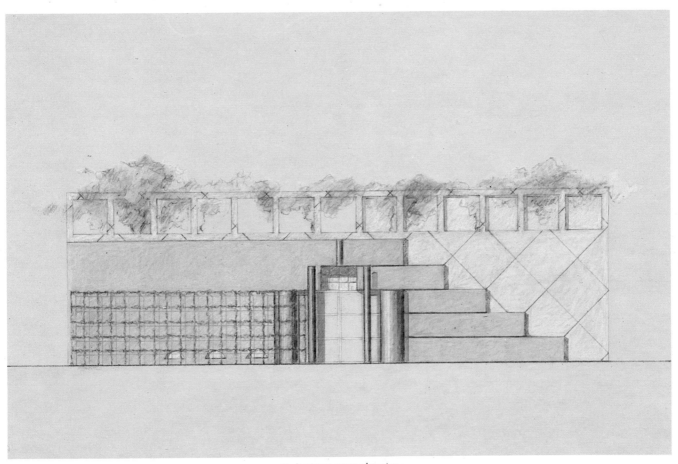

Preliminary street elevation

Preliminary south elevation

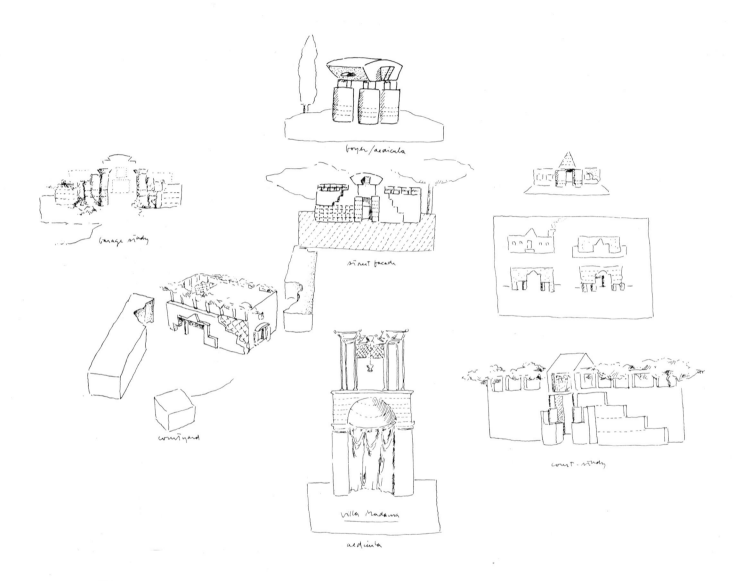

foyer/aedicula

garage study

street facade

courtyard

Villa Madama

aedicula

court-study

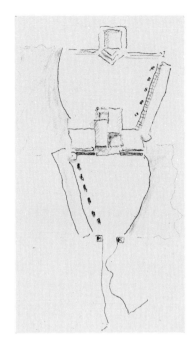
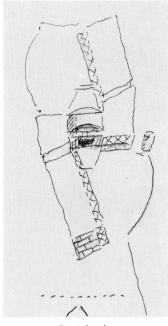
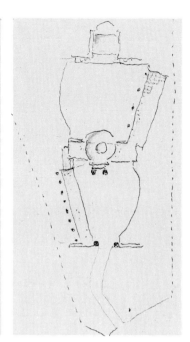

Parti sketches

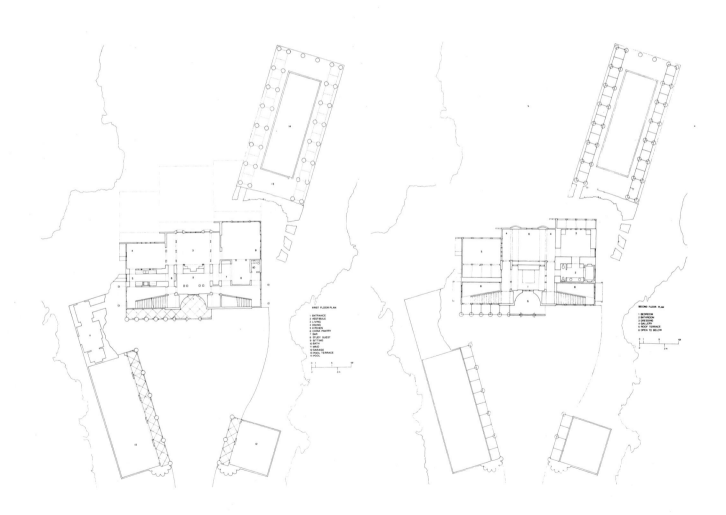

First floor plan   *Second floor plan*

Model view of the forecourt and street facade

Model view of the garden facade and pool

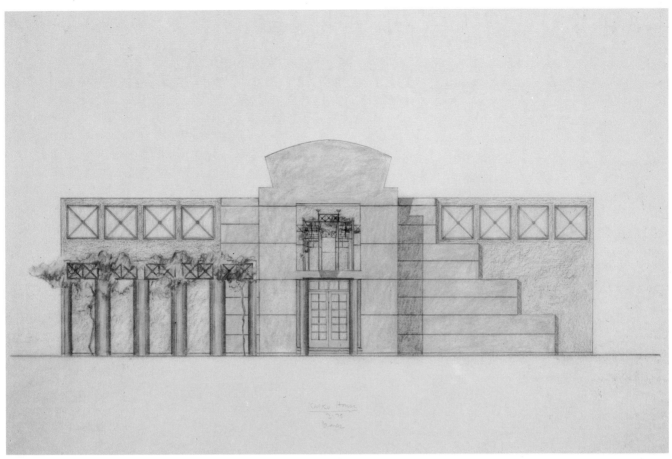

Street elevation

Preliminary garden elevation

Living room

Model view of the garden facade and pergola

1978

Vacation House
Aspen, Colorado

This large vacation house is designed to be used by a single family with frequent guests. As the house is not to be occupied year-round by the clients, it is also necessary to provide quarters for full-time caretakers.

The site is located at the confluence of two small rivers which become the primary influence on the location and orientation of the complex. The main house is oriented toward the south and faces one of the two rivers, while the guest house is oriented east and faces the other river. The two arms provide the basis for an organization around a central court. The third side of the court is made by staff quarters and storage buildings which flank the vehicular entrance. The fourth side gives access to the pool and orchard and offers a view to the mountains beyond.

The exterior wall surfaces of the building employ local wood log-cabin construction but reinterpret that vernacular within a more classical organization. The strong wooden base provides a visual link to the ground, while the remaining face of the building is seen as more ephemeral and analogous to the surrounding landscape. The center section of the building is capped by a roof that not only gives importance to the center mass but also provides a sense of enclosure within the great hall below.

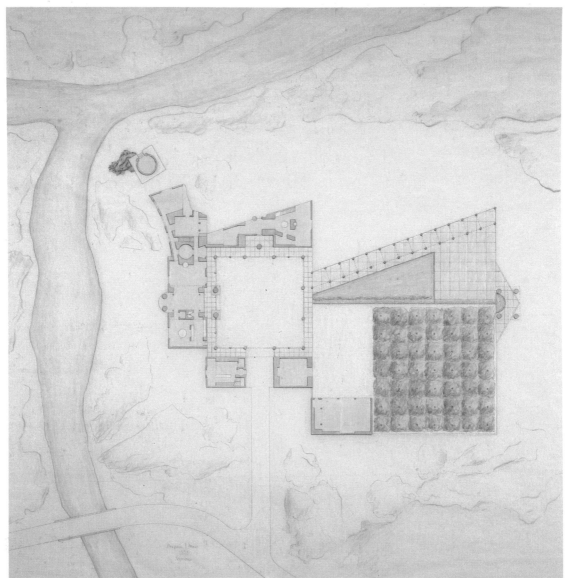

Site plan

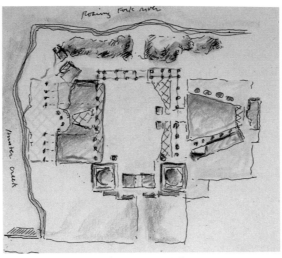

Preliminary site study

Overhead view of model

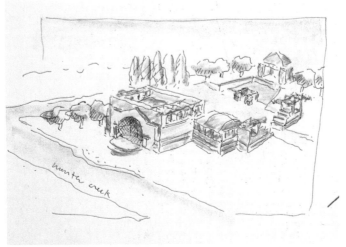

Preliminary study

Log cabin

Log cabin

Bandstand in Aspen, Colorado

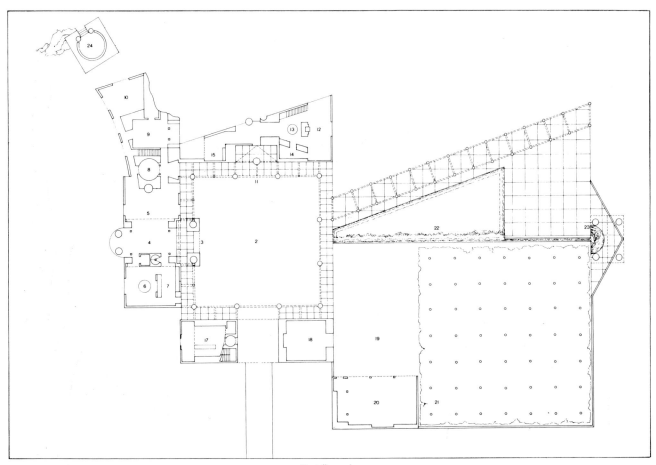

First floor plan

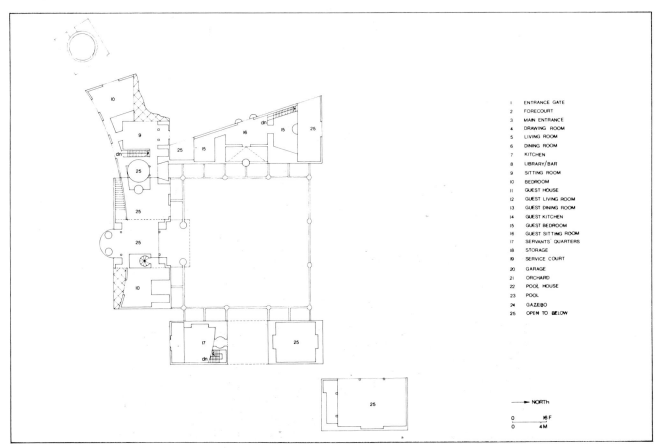

1	ENTRANCE GATE
2	FORECOURT
3	MAIN ENTRANCE
4	DRAWING ROOM
5	LIVING ROOM
6	DINING ROOM
7	KITCHEN
8	LIBRARY/BAR
9	SITTING ROOM
10	BEDROOM
11	GUEST HOUSE
12	GUEST LIVING ROOM
13	GUEST DINING ROOM
14	GUEST KITCHEN
15	GUEST BEDROOM
16	GUEST SITTING ROOM
17	SERVANTS' QUARTERS
18	STORAGE
19	SERVICE COURT
20	GARAGE
21	ORCHARD
22	POOL HOUSE
23	POOL
24	GAZEBO
25	OPEN TO BELOW

NORTH

Second floor plan

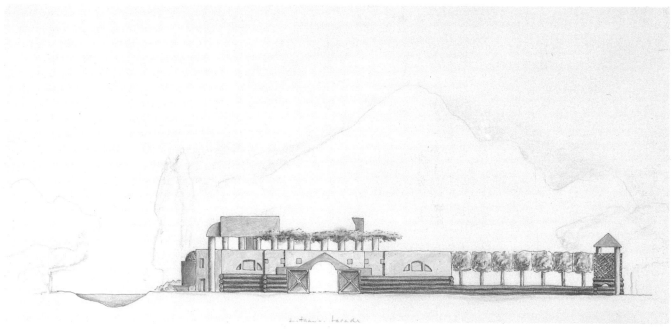

Entrance elevation

East view of model

South view of model

Hunter Creek elevation

Roaring Fork River elevation

West view of model

North view of model

Forecourt entrance elevation

variation on Schinkes
Casa Cenci near the villa Borghese
Rome

gazebo study

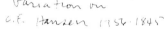
variation on
C.F. Hansen 1756-1845

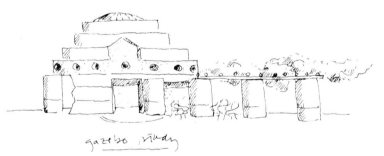

gazebo study

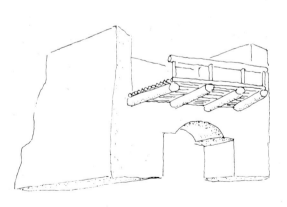

L. Hesse
1855

Fireplace studies

Hauserman Showroom
New York, New York

Wall gallery, elevation and plan

The Hauserman showroom was meant to demonstrate their various systems of movable walls. The showroom is located in an existing office building in New York with a good orientation to the views along Fifth Avenue. A thematic organization has allowed a chronological description of walls in general; though this does not become a "wall museum", it is nevertheless a way of bringing the company's current wall systems into an architectural and historical context. The various Hauserman systems are shown within the open field of the plan and are in themselves constructed to make rooms. There is a parallel exhibition of the wall and its uses in history within a thickened "window wall" which is "relieved" to allow the insertion of small showcases for plaster relief models of historical walls. This window wall allows passage behind it to encourage the view to the avenue as well as to temper the strong west light at that edge. The remaining wall surfaces of the showroom are "decorated" with photomurals of significant walls from the Modern Movement.

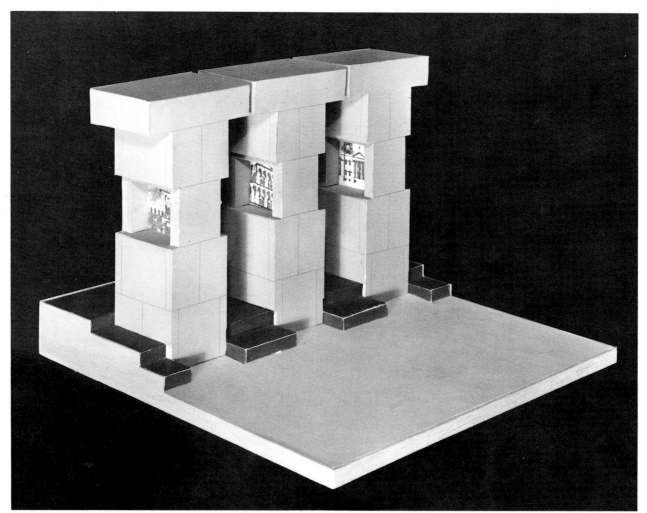

Wall gallery model

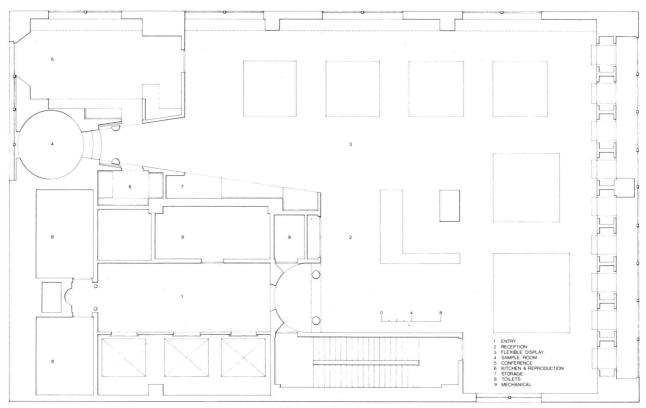

1   ENTRY
2   RECEPTION
3   FLEXIBLE DISPLAY
4   SAMPLE ROOM
5   CONFERENCE
6   KITCHEN & REPRODUCTION
7   STORAGE
8   TOILETS
9   MECHANICAL

Showroom floor plan

1978

French and Company
New York, New York

French & Company is known as an antique dealer in New York with a reputation for exquisite 17th and 18th century French and Italian antique furniture. The owner has purchased a townhouse on 65th Street in Manhattan which was built in the 1940's as a residence and which has since been greatly altered inside. The existing living room and solarium are to be used for the furniture showrooms, and the remainder of the building will be used as the owner's residence. Along with renovation of the interior, this project includes the addition of another floor at the top of the building, to be used as a roof terrace and greenhouse. This addition requires major changes in the facade structure and fenestration. The adjacent buildings vary in quality and size from a rather good turn-of-the-century Beaux Arts Palladian three-story residence on one side to an anonymous multistory apartment block on the other. An attempt has been made to continue the surfaces of the adjacent buildings across the new face. The new facade will be entered centrally, and the central figure of the entrance is in turn organized in a vertical three-part division of base, *piano nobile*, and upper or attic stories.

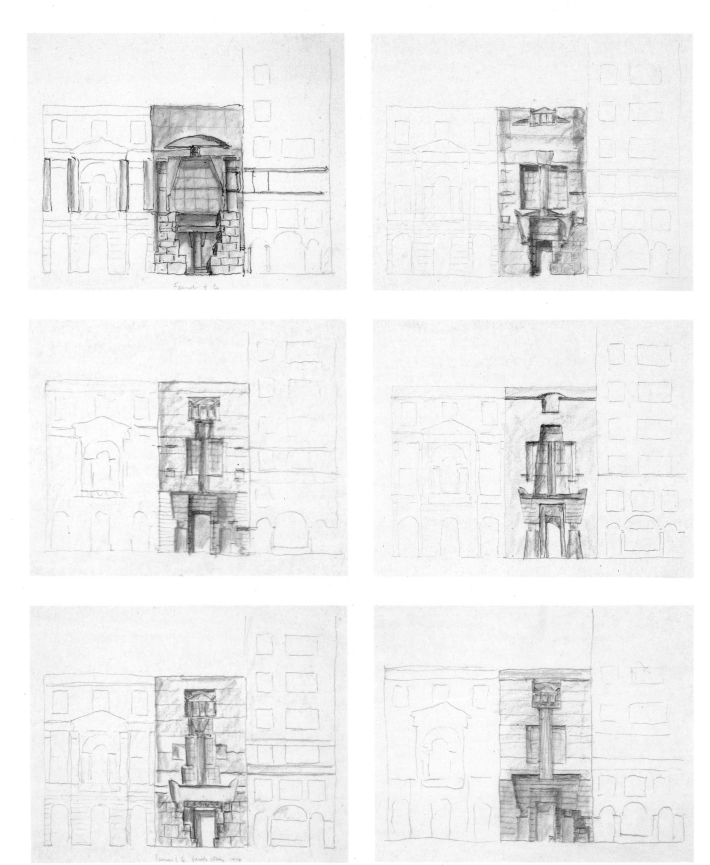

Facade studies

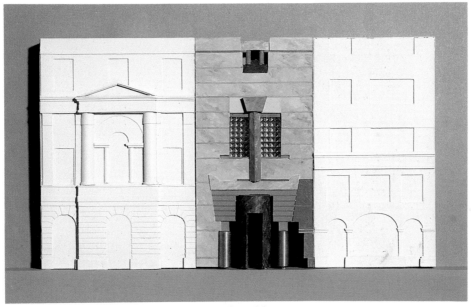

Facade model

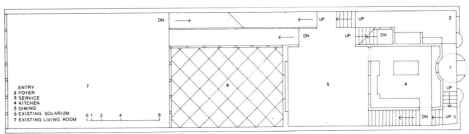

ENTRY
2 FOYER
3 SERVICE
4 KITCHEN
5 DINING
6 EXISTING SOLARIUM
7 EXISTING LIVING ROOM

First floor plan

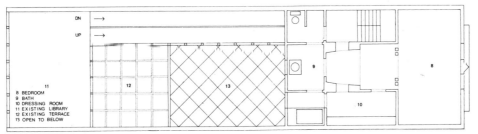

8 BEDROOM
9 BATH
10 DRESSING ROOM
11 EXISTING LIBRARY
12 EXISTING TERRACE
13 OPEN TO BELOW

Second floor plan

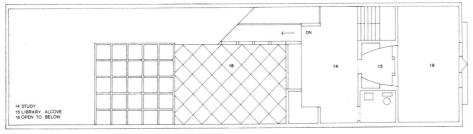

14 STUDY
15 LIBRARY ALCOVE
16 OPEN TO BELOW

Third floor plan

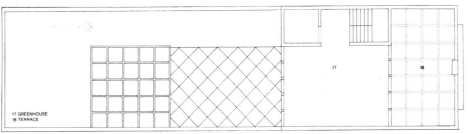

17 GREENHOUSE
18 TERRACE

Fourth floor plan

1978

Referential Sketches

These referential sketches were used as primary illustrations for an interview with Michael Graves published in 1980 in VIA (University of Pennsylvania).

1979

Sunar Furniture Showroom
New York, New York

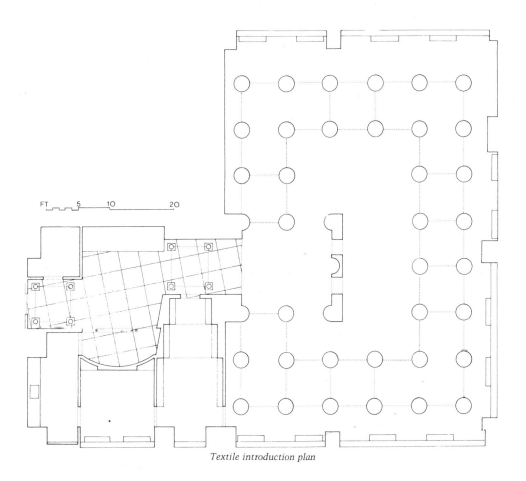

Textile introduction plan

The first showroom designed for Sunar, now dismantled, included a permanent section at the entrance, providing a foyer, vestibule, textile display room, manager's office and kitchen, which preceded a large open room for changing displays of Sunar's furniture and fabric lines. A mural, located in a curving niche in the vestibule, extends the interior by suggesting a view beyond to an "alternative landscape". The mural also contains foreground and middle ground elements germane to Sunar's furniture line. The pieces assembled in this painting depict the sitting position, in a Klismos chair, the horizontal position, in a first century Roman couch, and the standing position, with the artist's easel. The easel's surface also becomes a window to the garden whose mullion is a fragment of the plan of the showroom. The crank of the floor grid inflects ones movement from the entry toward the rear space through a four column pavilion or gate which also gives access to the fabric room to the right.

The initial display designed for the large room was for a textile introduction which took place at night. To engender the sense of light on the fabric, which was thought to enhance the natural surface quality of the fabric itself, a metaphorical garden was created, where the fabric was draped through lattice panels in a continous pergola around the room.

Mural in entry vestibule

Easel mural cartoon

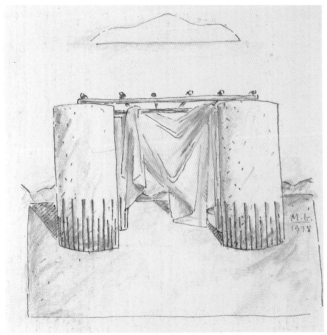

Pergola sketch

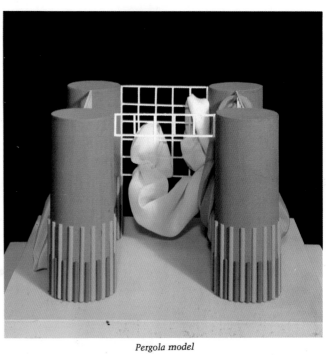

Pergola model

Entrance

Vestibule

Entrance to textile room

1978

Railroad Station Addition and Renovation
New Jersey

View of model from the street

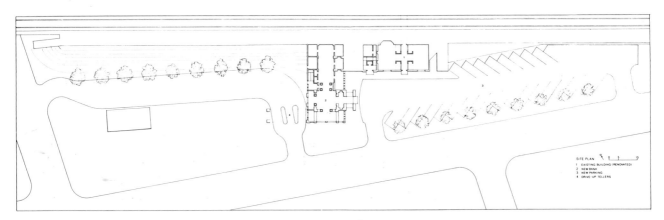

The existing railroad station, built in 1906, is to be renovated and an office wing, including a branch bank, will be added to it. The new building is located perpendicular to the existing structure and connected to it through an existing stair wing which will be enclosed. The new L-shaped scheme responds to the requirements for access to the drive-in tellers windows on the west side of the building. At the same time, its L-shaped configuration suggests the enclosure of an automobile forecourt in front of the station, serving as a drop-off point for the station and the newly renovated offices above.

The court facades are made complimentary or compatible by continuing the three-part organization (base, middle, and top) of the existing building's facade across the new building, particularly at the rusticated base. The three main entrances to the buildings—one to the train, one to the lobby for the second floor offices, and one to the first floor bank located in the addition—have each been given their own identities.

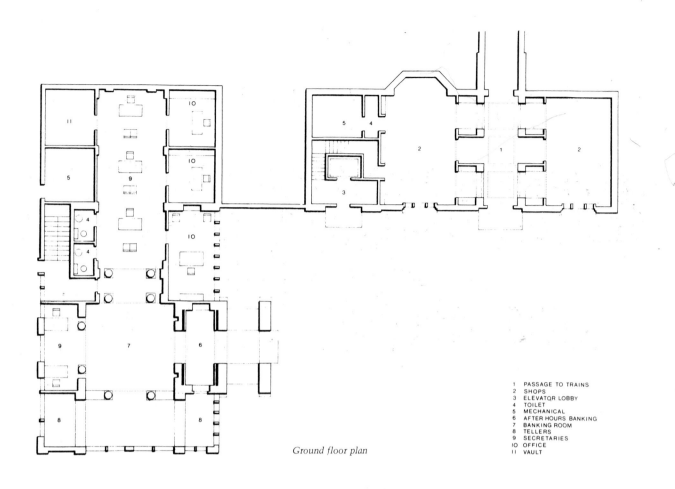

Ground floor plan

1 PASSAGE TO TRAINS
2 SHOPS
3 ELEVATOR LOBBY
4 TOILET
5 MECHANICAL
6 AFTER HOURS BANKING
7 BANKING ROOM
8 TELLERS
9 SECRETARIES
10 OFFICE
11 VAULT

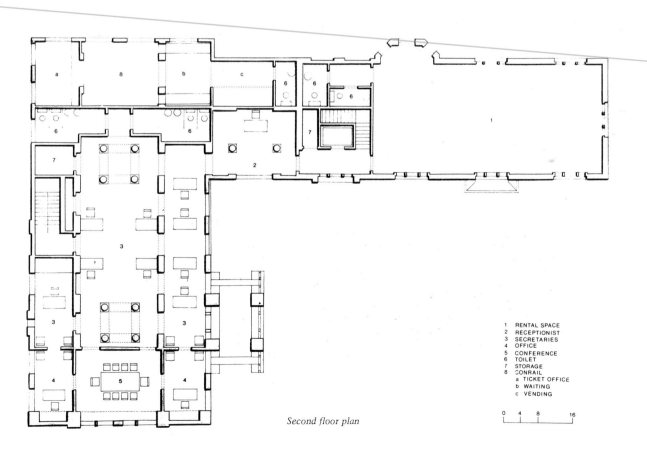

Second floor plan

1 RENTAL SPACE
2 RECEPTIONIST
3 SECRETARIES
4 OFFICE
5 CONFERENCE
6 TOILET
7 STORAGE
8 CONRAIL
  a TICKET OFFICE
  b WAITING
  c VENDING

0 4 8 16

Courtyard view of model

Northwest view of model

Model view of forecourt and bank entrance

Existing railroad station

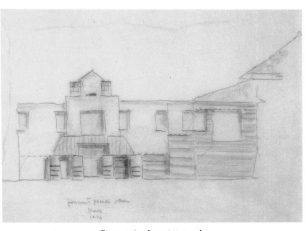

Forecourt elevation study

Folded out elevation of forecourt, bank entrance and railroad station

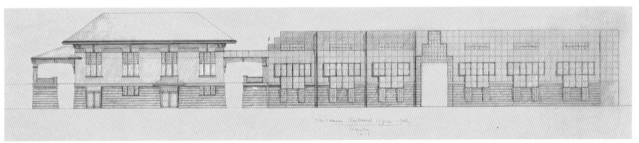

Preliminary street elevation

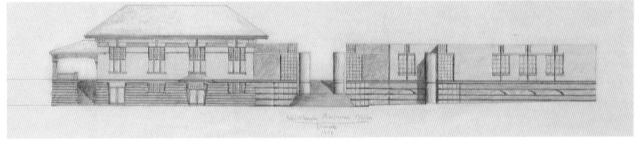

Preliminary street elevation

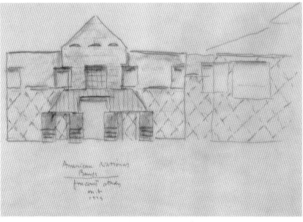

Forecourt elevation study

Forecourt elevation study

Railroad Station Addition and Renovation

Folded out elevation of forecourt, bank entrance and railroad station

Section through renovation and addition

Street (southwest) elevation

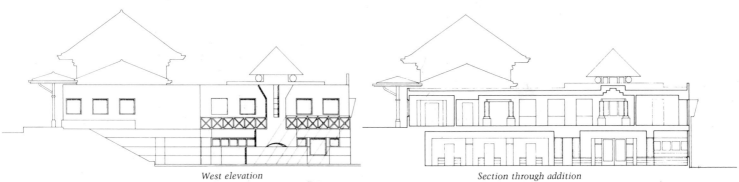

West elevation

Section through addition

1979

Sunar Furniture Showroom
Temporary Installation
Los Angeles, California

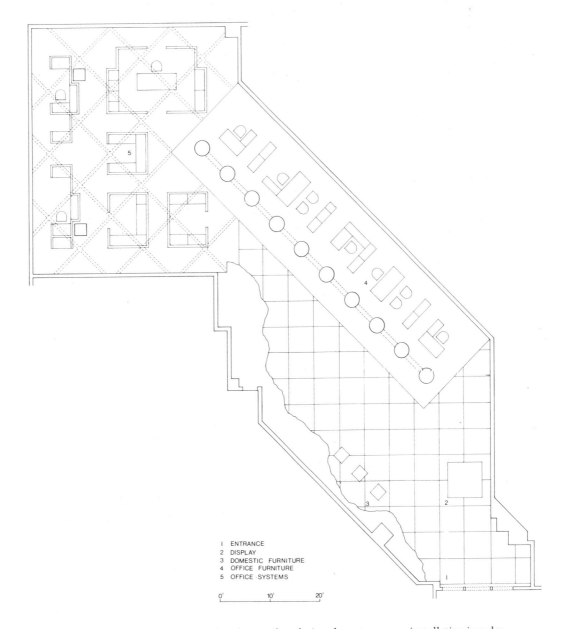

1 ENTRANCE
2 DISPLAY
3 DOMESTIC FURNITURE
4 OFFICE FURNITURE
5 OFFICE SYSTEMS

0'   10'   20'

The Sunar furniture showroom in Los Angeles was first designed as a temporary installation in order that the clients could introduce their furniture to the western market as soon as possible. Given an awkward periphery and a difficult angle of entry in the existing space, an attempt was made to supply some legibility to the plan by using a wall of drapery which allows the furniture to be seen more on its own terms than with the curiosities of the surrounding surfaces. Non-structural columns, which carry lines of light, and chair-rails draped with fabric from the client's textile collection are used as boundaries between domestic and office furniture and office systems.

Passage along pergola

Fabric display

Furniture display

Cover Design

Cover design for Progressive Architecture Magazine

1977-1981

Furniture Designs

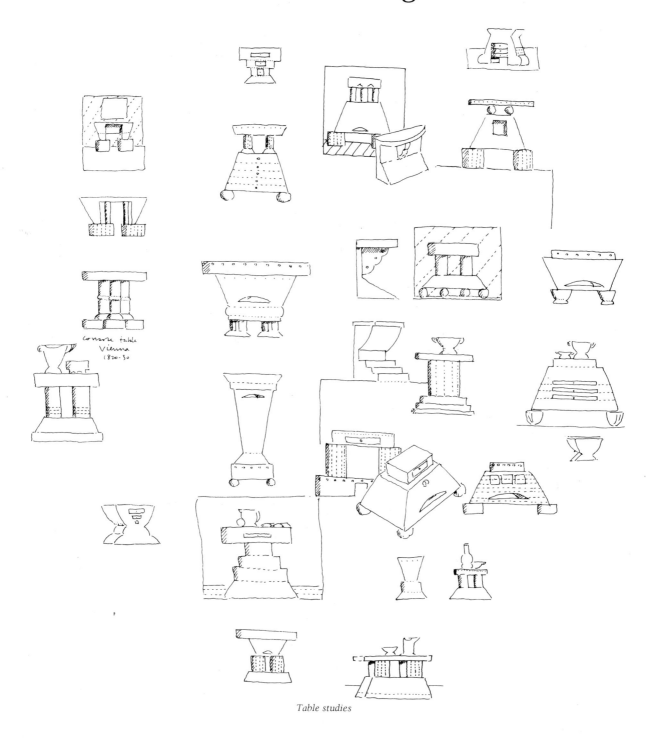

Table studies

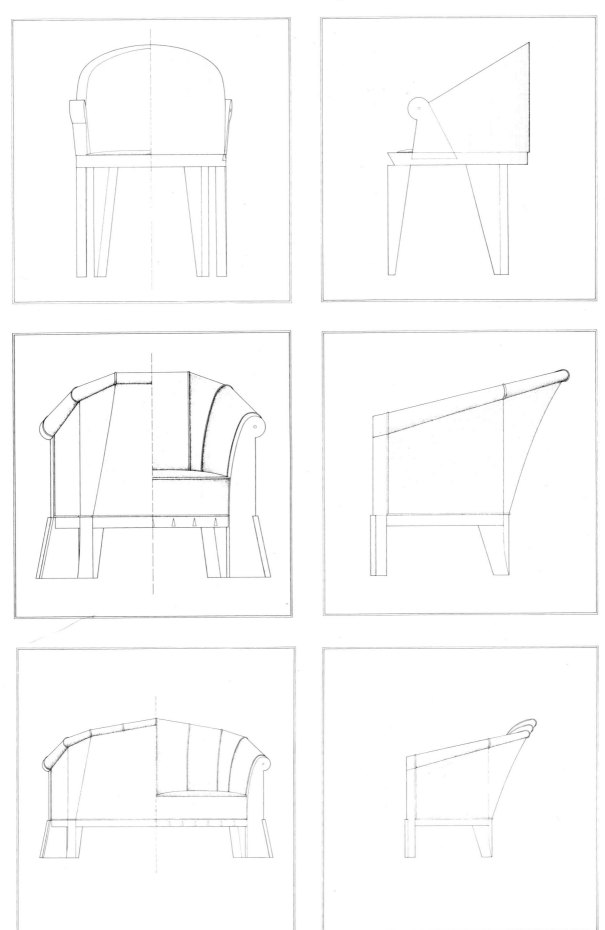

Side chair, lounge chair and settee

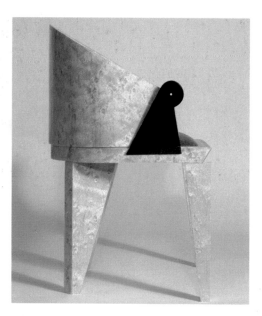

Side chair and lounge chair

Table prototypes

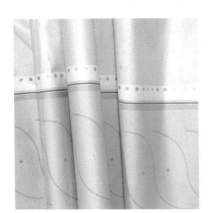

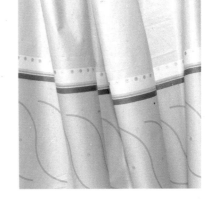

Casement fabric designs

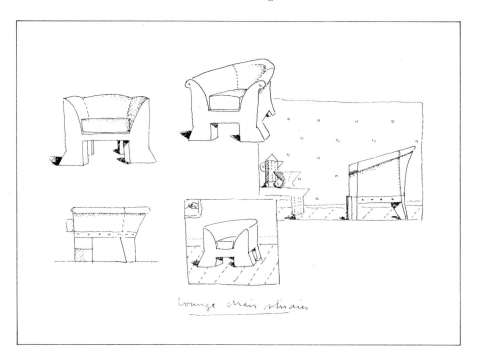

lounge chair studies

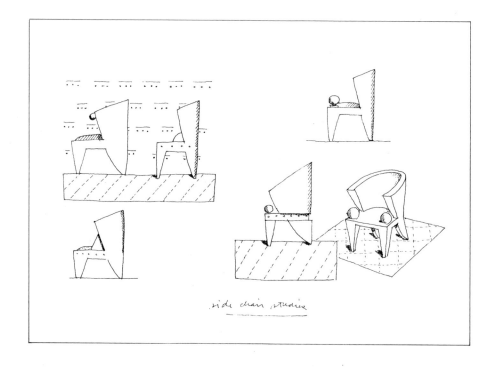

side chair studies

1979

Sunar Furniture Showroom
Chicago, Illinois

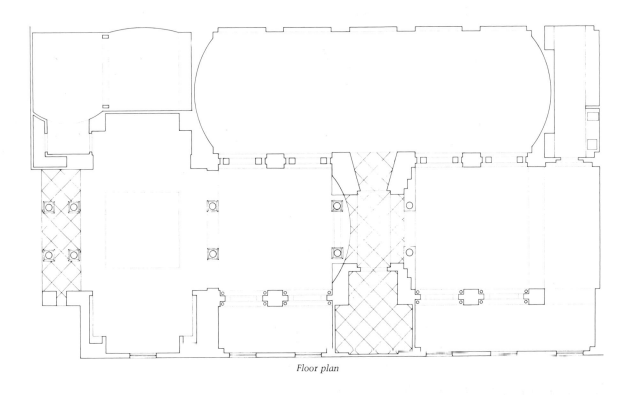

Floor plan

The Sunar furniture showroom in the Merchandise Mart in Chicago attempts to offset the problem of an inside space denied natural light by suggesting a metaphorical street by which one understands the showroom as a series of spaces, rooms, or even shops on that street. The street association or suggestion allows the outside edges to be described by windows which give visual access to the assembled furniture groups inside. These groups are assembled in a progression from the relatively small scale of fabric to domestic scaled furniture along the main axis, to Sunar's office systems displayed in a large open space reached by a cross-axis. It was thought that by making both centralized enclosures and linear organizations ranging in size from small to large, a variety of settings would be suggested to the observer. The primary axis from the entrance to the showroom moves through a series of four such spaces and is completed by the figure of Terminus, a low relief painted construction. The mythological figure of Terminus is used here to suggest a thematic completion of the axis from the street to the end of the internal space.

Office furniture display room

Entry   *Column detail*

Entry looking toward "Terminus"

"Terminus" wall construction study

"Terminus" wall construction

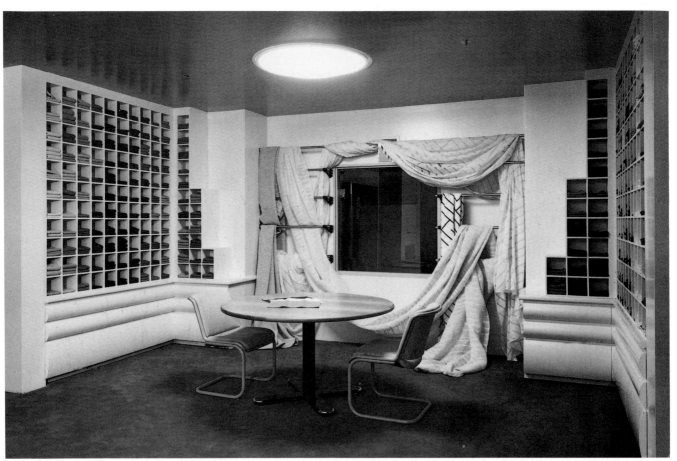

Fabric display room

View into the showroom from the corridor

Entry to office systems display

1979

Beach House
Loveladies, New Jersey

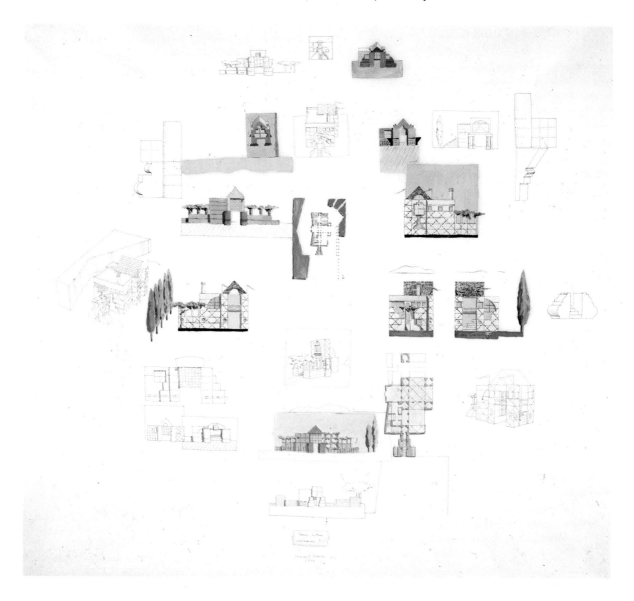

The beach house is designed as a summer house for two adults and occasional guests. The building is sited to insure the best view of the bay from the southwest corner and to orient the house to prevailing breezes. The clients expect to spend their time primarily on the lattice-roofed porch and the open deck, and therefore this section of the house becomes significant in the design strategy. The porch pavilion is engaged to the house as an extension of the living room and yet is also seen as part of the garden as a gazebo with lattice roof and corner window seats. Because of the pavilion's centralized configuration within an organization which includes both building and garden, the house itself can be read as a fragment of a larger scheme.

Local site regulations require that the ground floor of all buildings be elevated to above five feet, and therefore this two-story building appears more vertical than one would normally expect. The height requirement has been offset by the horizontal extension into the landscape. It was thought that the strategy employed, that of a greater development of the site, might keep this tiny house (1500 square feet) from appearing as one more centralized object in the center of its own suburban turf.

Preliminary facade studies

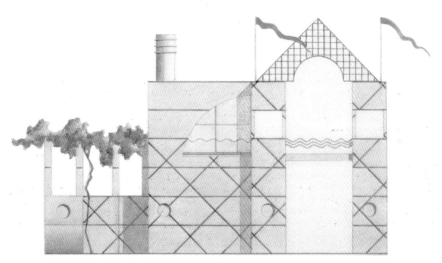

West elevation

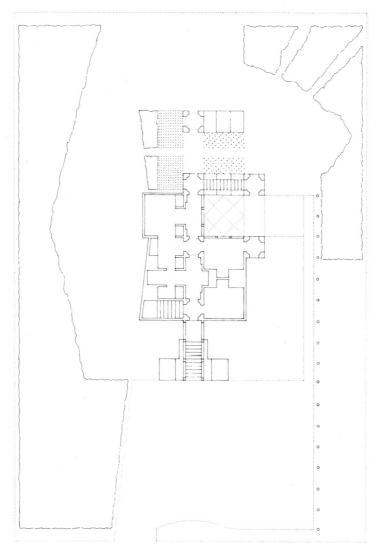

Site plan

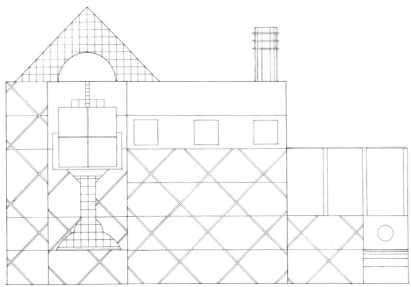

East elevation

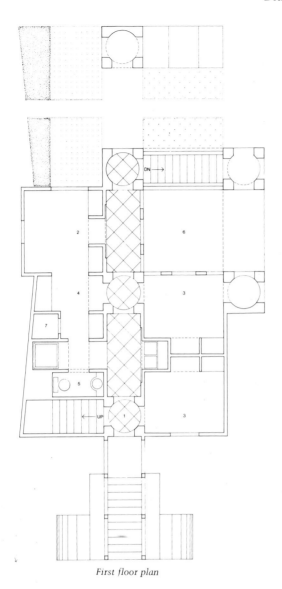

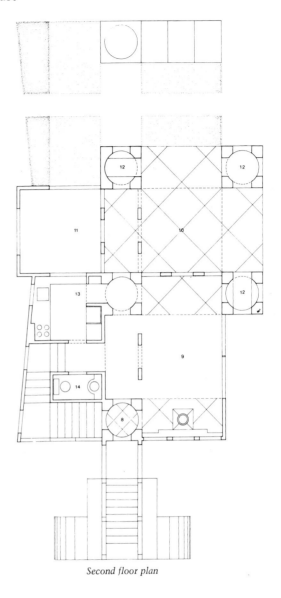

First floor plan

Second floor plan

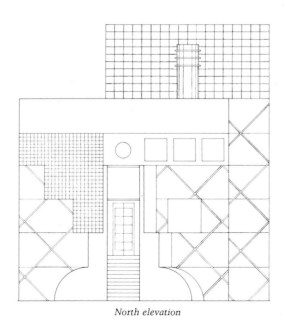

North elevation

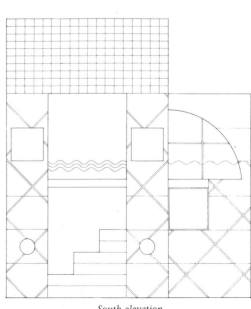

South elevation

Northwest view of model

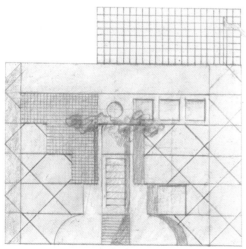

North elevation

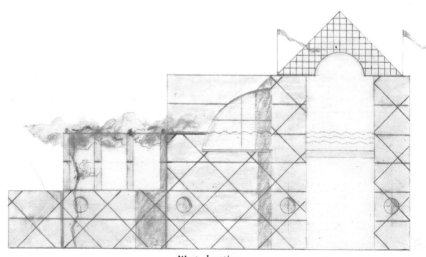

West elevation

Southeast view of model

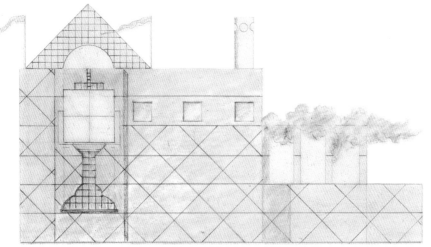

East elevation

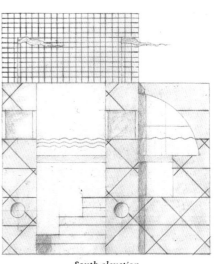

South elevation

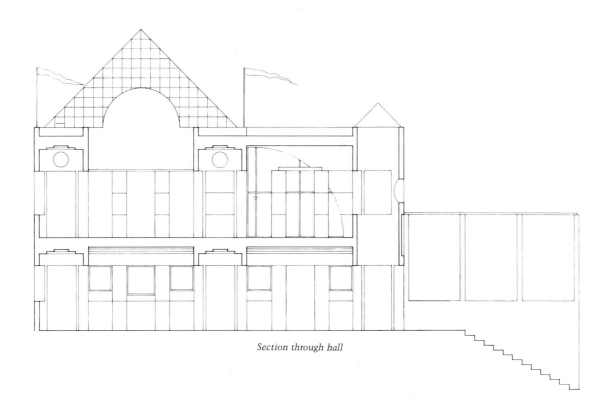

Section through hall

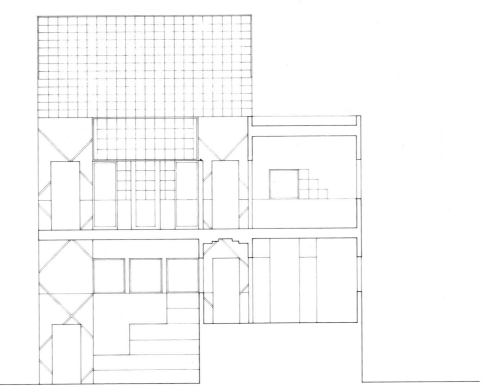

Section through deck

Preliminary study

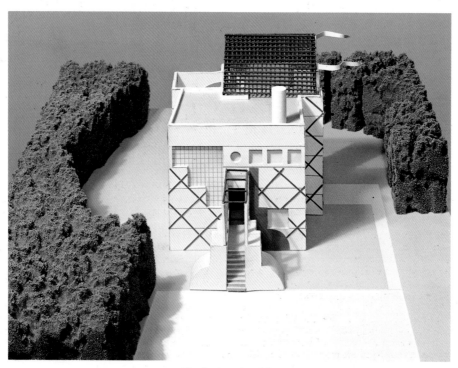

North view of model

1979

"Buildings for Best Products"
Exhibition
New York, New York

Entrance

As the theoretical and historical basis for this project, ideas about traditional forms of commercial organization were examined, particularly the Greek stoa. One of the most important aspects of the stoa as a type is that it encourages the most favorable form of shopping, that of a linear progression, where one can examine at close range the goods at hand.

In the shopping districts which have typically been developed in the extended city, namely in its strips and suburbs, the car and its parking requirements become another important consideration. The development of these shopping districts is characterized by the mall plans where shopping activities ring an internal void and turn their backs on the surrounding parking lots. The result of this pattern is an erosion of the street in favor of enormous parking fields with occasional shopping centers growing from their midst.

This project for Best Products proposes that the presence of the car be admitted as a significant and symbolic aspect of the suburb. The shopping center in its current development is here turned inside out, so that one parks in the central ''agora'' or mall and shops at its edge, along the line of the stoa. The dimension of the facade of the standard box building, which was given as the starting point for this project, has been extended by a covered pergola, and a second line is established along the street, with signage pavilions identifying the primary tenant.

Entrance

Shopping arcade

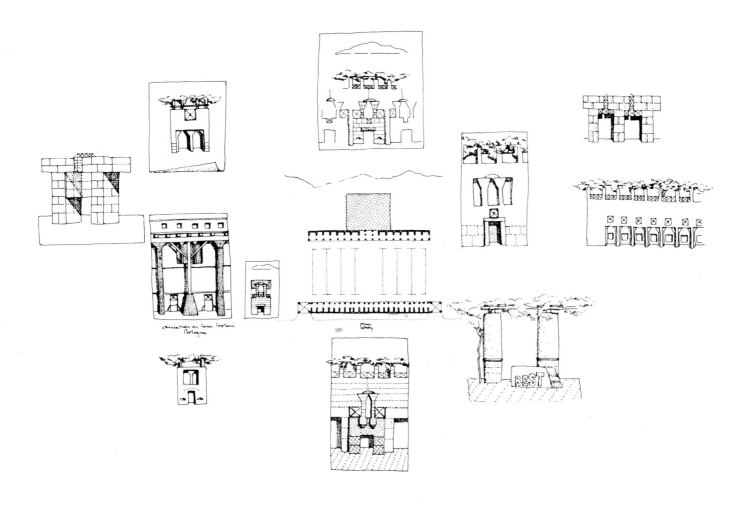

Entrance

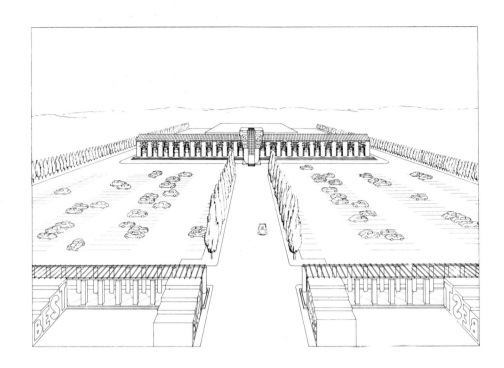

Entrance facade

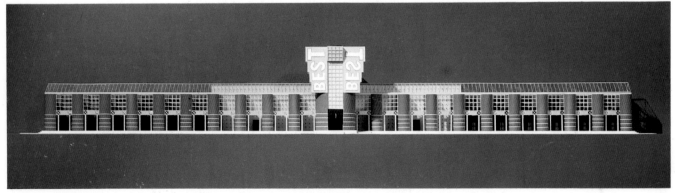

Entrance facade

1980

The Portland Building
Portland, Oregon

Fifth Avenue elevation

The Portland Building was a design-build competition sponsored by the city of Portland, Oregon. Located on a 200-foot square downtown block, the building will house the city's municipal offices. This particular site offers a rich and special setting characterized by the adjacent City Hall and County Courthouse buildings on two sides, and the public transit mall and the park on the other two sides.

The design of the building addresses the public nature of both the urban context and the internal program. In order to reinforce the building's associative or mimetic qualities, the facades are organized in a classical three-part division of base, middle or body, and attic or head. The large paired columns on the main facades act as a portal or gate and reinforce one's sense of passage through the building along its main axis, from Fourth to Fifth Avenues. The most publicly accessible activities are placed in the base of the building which is colored light green in reference to the ground. The base of the building also reinforces the importance of the street as an essential urban form by providing a loggia on three sides and shopping along the sidewalk on the fourth.

The city services are located in the middle section of the building, behind a large window of reflective glass which both accepts and mirrors the city itself and which symbolizes the collective, public nature of the activities held within. The figure of Lady Commerce from the city seal, reinterpreted to represent a broader cultural tradition and renamed "Portlandia," is placed in front of one of the large windows as a further reference to the city.

Above the city offices, the five tenant floors are located behind a lintel-like surface which is seen as supported on the large columns. On the top floor, a balcony overlooks the commercial center to the east and a public pavilion supported on a sconce on the west side offers a distant view to Mount Hood.

While the side streets of Madison and Main are by nature less active than Fourth or Fifth Avenues, their large colonnades support the idea of the building as passage from commerce to park. The columns are tied together and embellished by garlands, a classical gesture of welcome thematically related to the wreath carried by Portlandia.

195

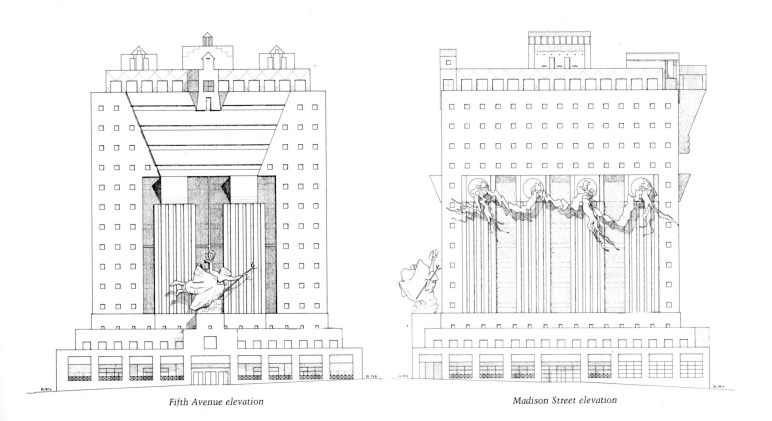

Fifth Avenue elevation

Madison Street elevation

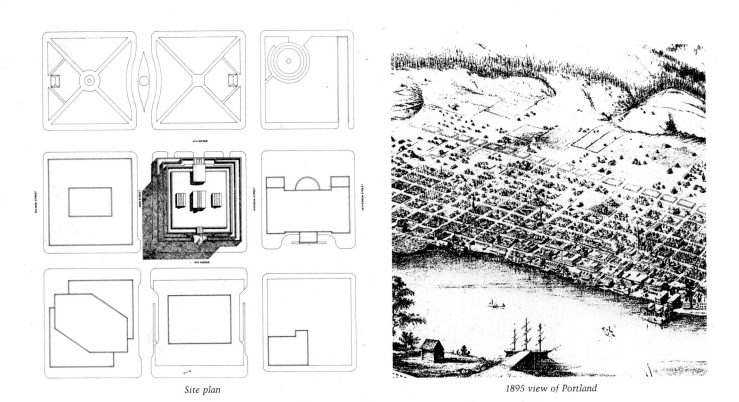

Site plan

1895 view of Portland

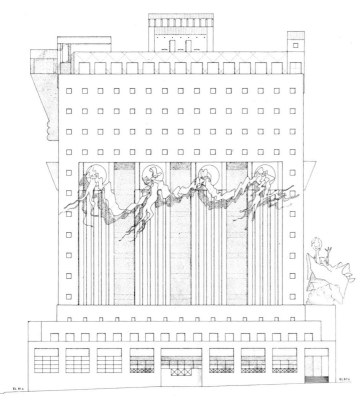

Main Street elevation

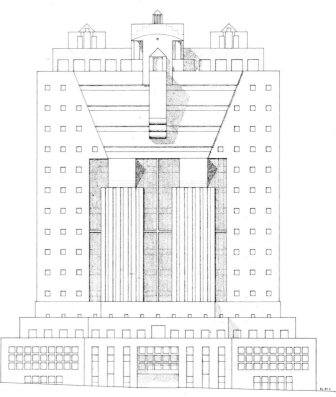

Fourth Avenue elevation

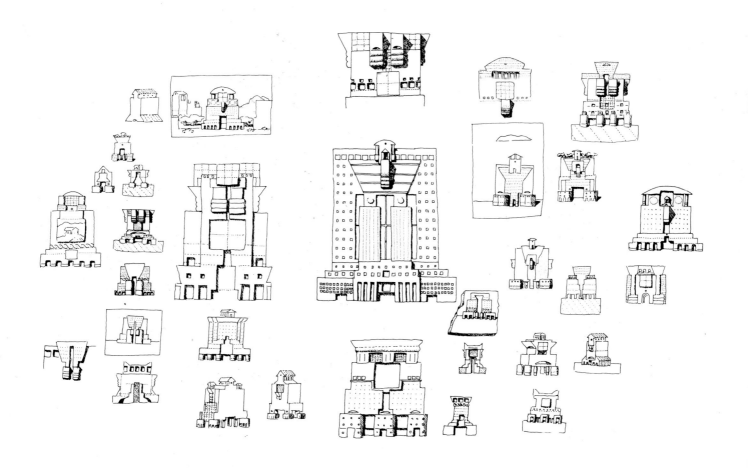

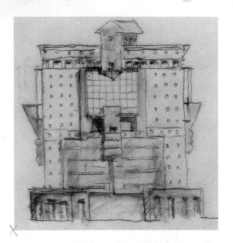
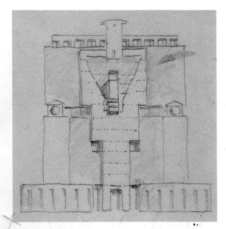
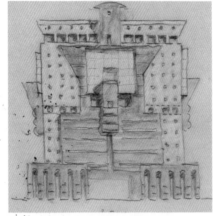
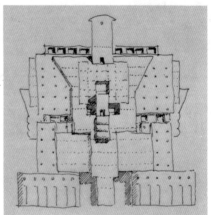

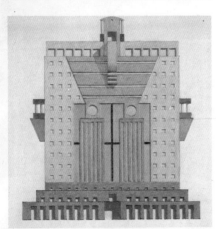

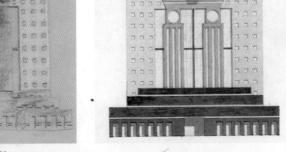

Facade studies

View from the park

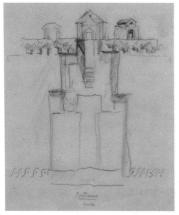

Facade study

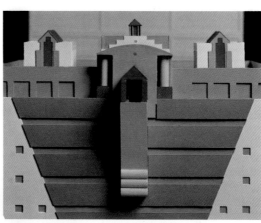

Detail of roof

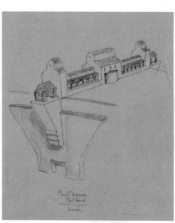

Penthouse study

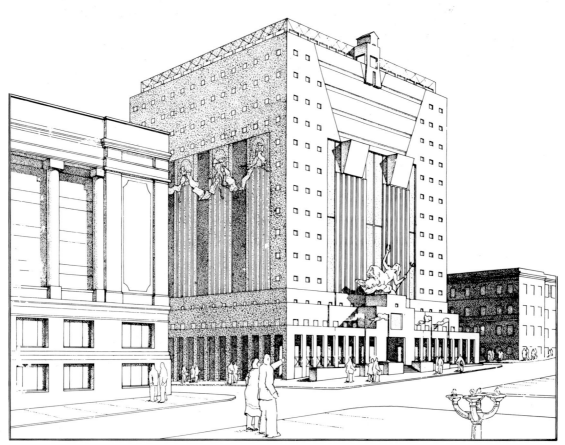

View from Fifth Avenue

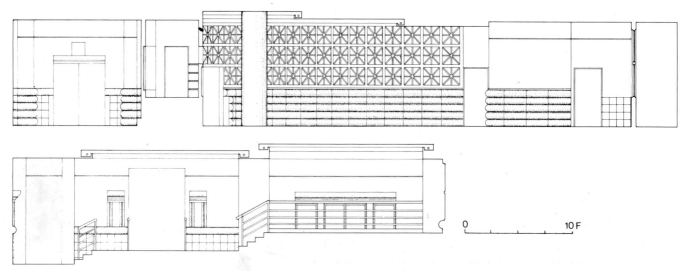

0   10 F

Section view: 4th Avenue Lobby, cafe and hearing room

200

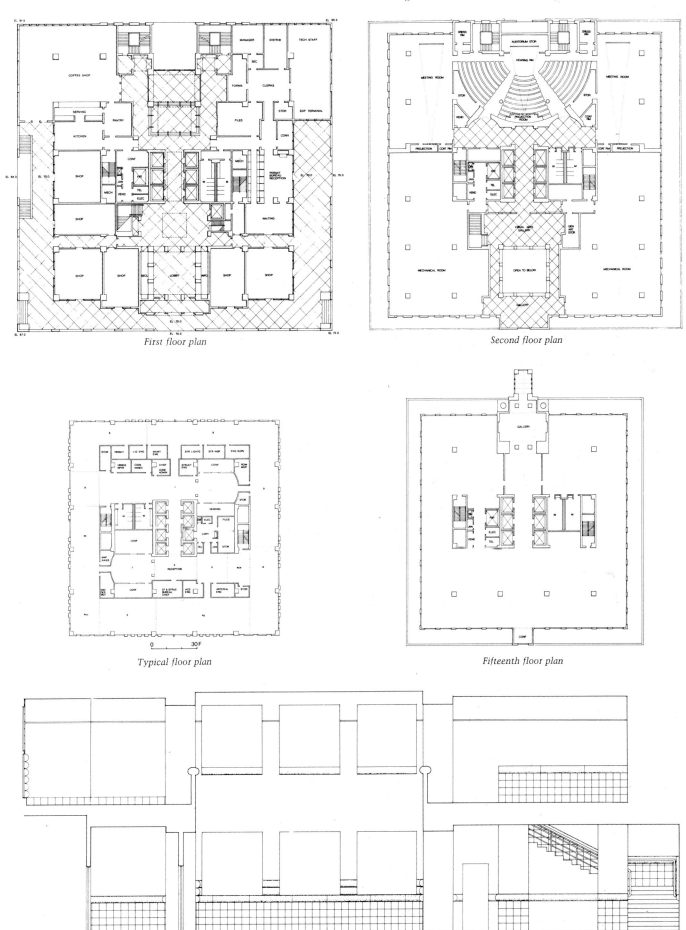

First floor plan

Second floor plan

Typical floor plan

Fifteenth floor plan

Section view: 5th Avenue Lobby and Visual Arts Gallery

Model view from Fourth Avenue

Model view from Fifth Avenue

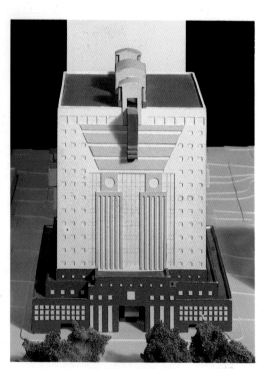

Preliminary model

Preliminary model

View from Fifth Avenue

Madison Avenue facade study

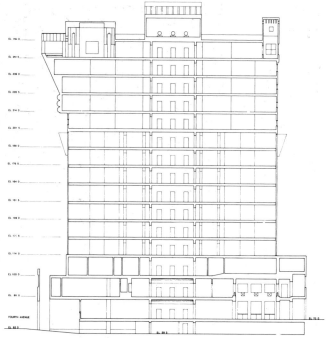

Building section

Garland study model

Garland study model

Lobby cafe

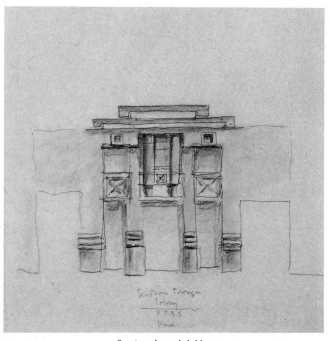

Section through lobby

View from Fifth Avenue

1979 and 1980

Rugs

Rug #1, 5' × 7'

The rug assumes a rather special design problem in that it is seen horizontally, somewhat the way one might look at a diagram or a floor plan. Though the rug has an image or object-value, it is not understood as most objects which are seen in the round or frontally. This rug was not meant as a tapestry or a wall hanging, but one which would be used in its traditional horizontal role. It was intriguing to deal with an object which does not have a top or bottom, in other words, which does not assume a role in gravity in the way we think of most objects, and therefore, like some De Stijl compositions, it had to be understood or accessible from all sides with a measure of equity.

In contrast to the neutrality of most modern floors, the rug offers the chance to develop the volume or three-dimenstional quality of space in that its colors and forms enhance the ideas of depth and distance. The colors used help to develop the figurative and associative values we might expect within the natural world. As aspects of nature are referred to in the "ground" or floor surface, we understand our location relative not only to the interior but also to the idea of the interior as an extended garden.

These rugs were designed to be woven by V'Soske.

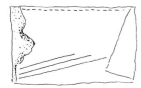 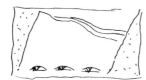  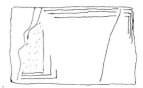

Rug #2, 8′ ×10′

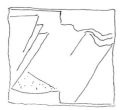

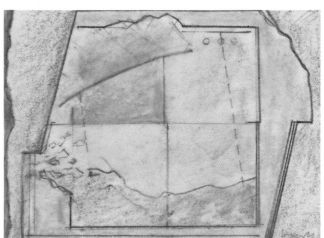

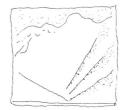

Rug studies

1980

Red River Valley Heritage Interpretive Center
Moorhead, Minnesota

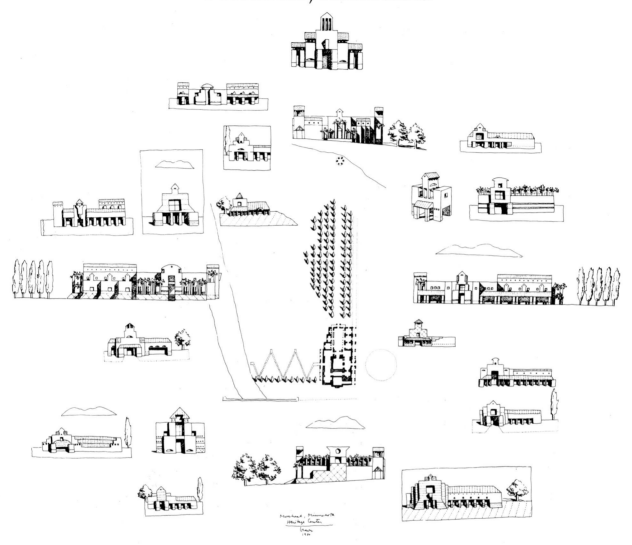

The Red River Valley Heritage Interpretive Center is the first component of the Fargo-Moorhead Cultural Center Bridge master plan to be developed. One of the most important aspects of the Interpretive Center is its particular urban setting in that the building is located in a garden at the edge of the Red River. Within the boundaries of both Fargo and Moorhead, it suggests complementary themes inherent in urban and rural life, both of which are part of this institution.

The building itself is organized in a way which supports the thematic continuity and linearity of the story to be told. Upon entering, one is given the option of attending a presentation in the central lecture hall or beginning the exhibition sequence in the loop of gallery spaces around it. The configuration of the galleries, which have frequent window access to the exterior, allows one to orient oneself easily within the organization as a whole. This relationship of the building to the outdoors is thematically important to an institution which helps to describe and educate us relative to our beginnings on the land.

In addition to the primary exhibition spaces which offer a variety of sizes and light qualities, space for traveling shows is located on the second floor. Also on this floor arranged around the central core, are the administrative offices, conference rooms, and the library and oral history collections.

The facades of the Interpretive Center reflect the special character of the buildng as an urban institution in a rural setting. It is in this purposeful double reading that the culture of man and his roots, both urban and rural, are further expressed.

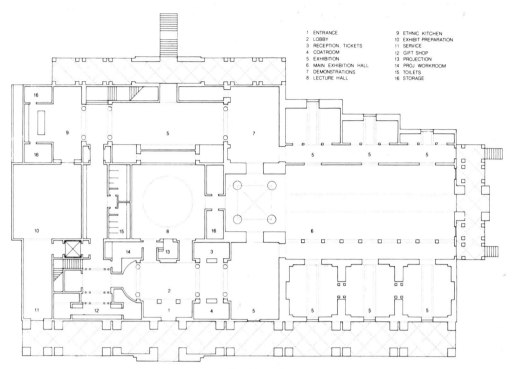

1   ENTRANCE
2   LOBBY
3   RECEPTION, TICKETS
4   COATROOM
5   EXHIBITION
6   MAIN EXHIBITION HALL
7   DEMONSTRATIONS
8   LECTURE HALL
9   ETHNIC KITCHEN
10 EXHIBIT PREPARATION
11 SERVICE
12 GIFT SHOP
13 PROJECTION
14 PROJ WORKROOM
15 TOILETS
16 STORAGE

First floor plan

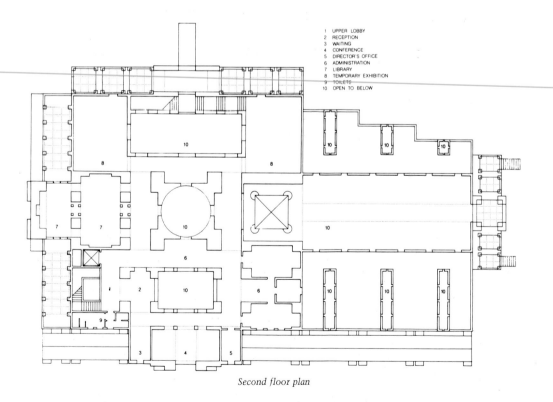

1   UPPER LOBBY
2   RECEPTION
3   WAITING
4   CONFERENCE
5   DIRECTOR'S OFFICE
6   ADMINISTRATION
7   LIBRARY
8   TEMPORARY EXHIBITION
9   TOILETS
10 OPEN TO BELOW

Second floor plan

Entrance elevation

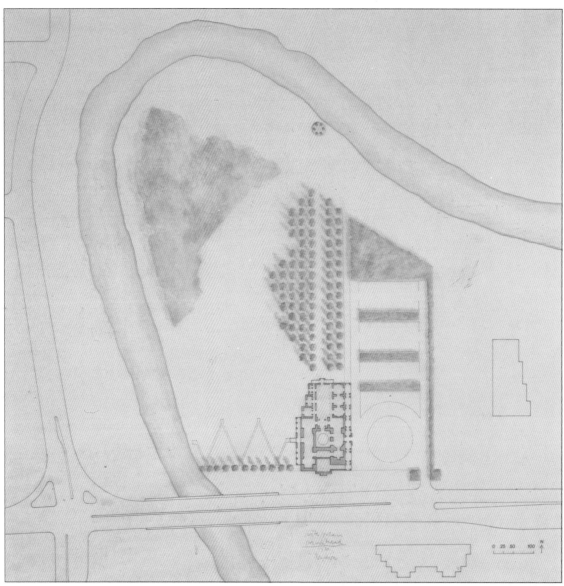

Site plan

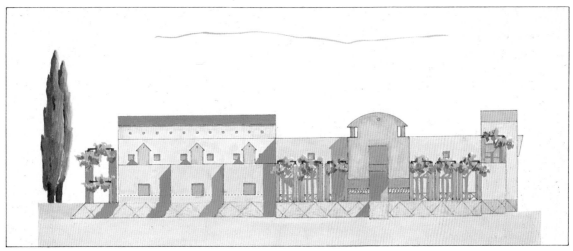

River elevation

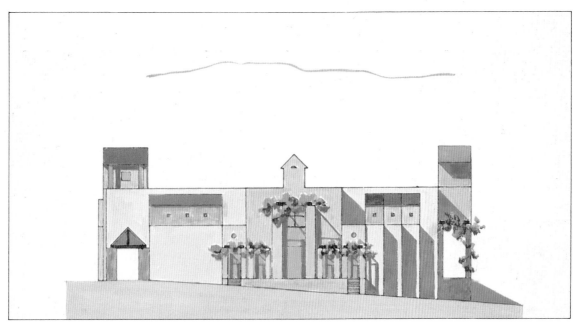

Garden elevation

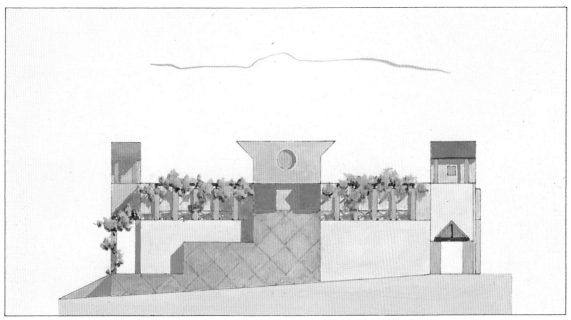

Highway elevation

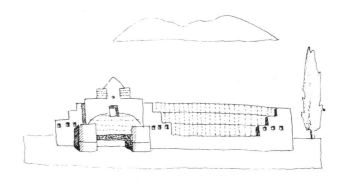
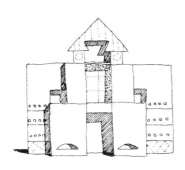
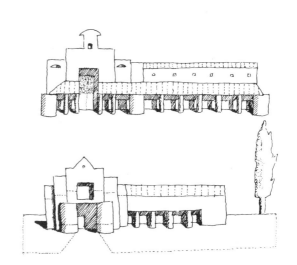
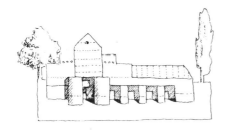
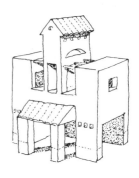
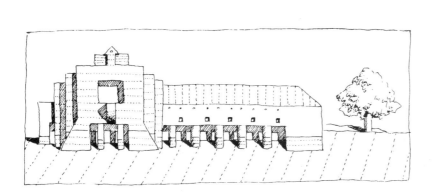

1979

Murals

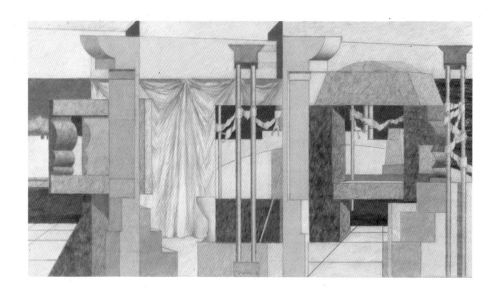

Cartoons for "Alternative Landscape" murals, Associated Metals and Minerals, New York, New York

Detail, John Witherspoon School mural, Princeton, New Jersey

John Witherspoon School mural

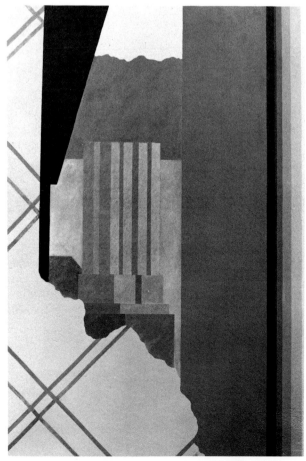

Mural detail

Mural detail

1980

Corporate Headquarters Competition
D.O.M.–Sicherheitstechnik
Bruhl, West Germany

Entrance court facade

DOM-Sicherheitstechnik, a West German manufacturer of security products, requires a new headquarters, office building, and training center for its 800 employees. This building will be added to the existing manufacturing plant and other low-lying outbuildings in the industrial park where it is located.

In organizing the functional and symbolic ideas of this building, the existing context has been used as a generator for the new additions. Given the existing setting, it is possible, through additions, to make greater use of the original building configuration; the additions are organized so as to provide the exterior spaces with a sense of enclosure, thus creating "rooms" within the open site.

The headquarters building is organized internally by a central space which gives symbolic focus to the entire complex. The Reception Hall, as the space for communal congregation, is given a height appropriate to its use and views into this space are allowed from the various office levels above. The Reception Hall, Products Display, and Cafeteria are located to take advantage of the new garden to the south. This garden in turn gives access to a larger lawn which flanks the present DOM building. The verticality of the new addition allows the complex to be visible and identified from the distant landscape.

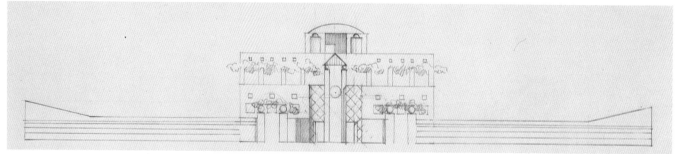

Street facade

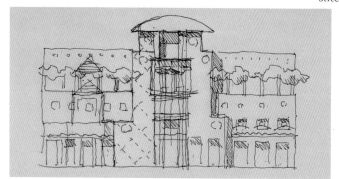

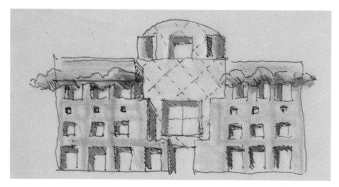

Entrance court facade studies

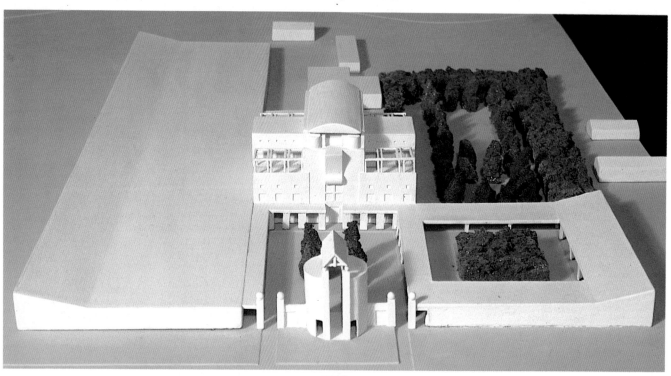

Model

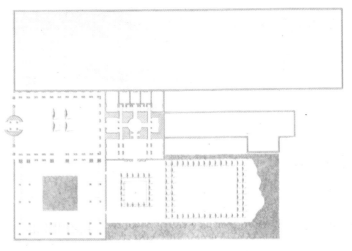

Site plan

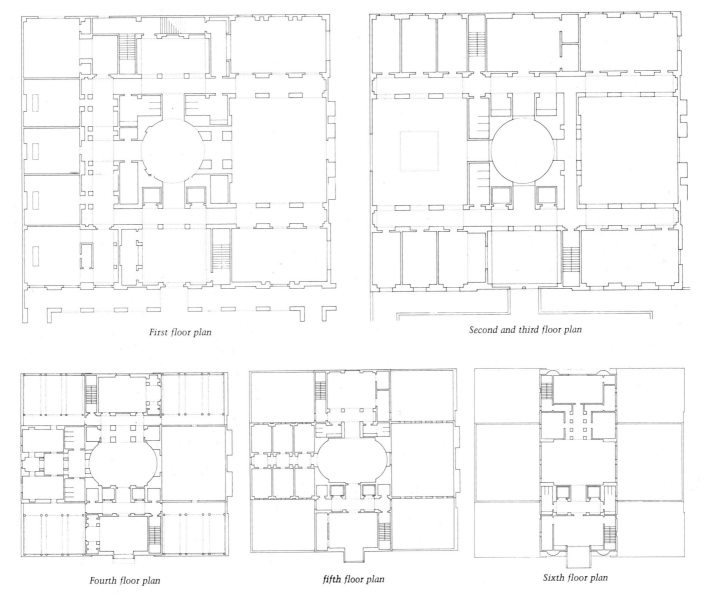

First floor plan

Second and third floor plan

Fourth floor plan

fifth floor plan

Sixth floor plan

Garden court

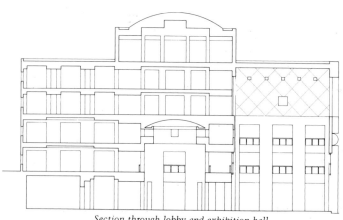

Section through lobby and exhibition hall

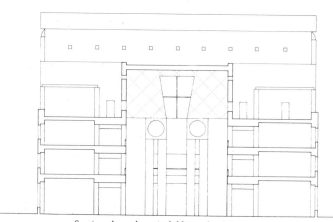

Section through main lobby and exhibition rooms

Entrance elevation

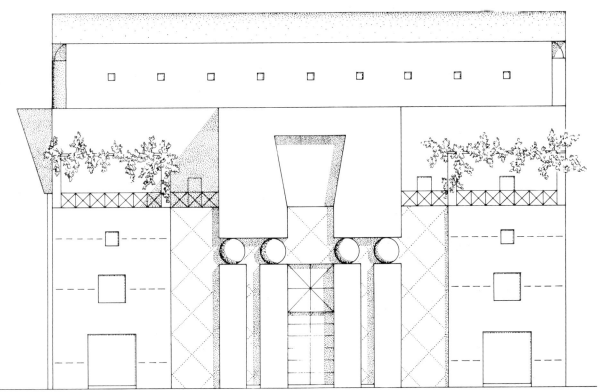

Garden elevation

1980

Sunar Furniture Showroom
Houston, Texas

Mural: "Alternative Landscape"

Mural cartoon

The showroom is organized so as to offer a variety of spatial sequences, accommodating various pieces of furniture and office systems, and emphasizing passage from one set of spaces to another. From the entry foyer, one passes along a "loggia" or circulation spine which organizes the larger and smaller spaces containing office systems and more domestically scaled furniture. Changes in ceiling height, surface textures, and lighting encourage the reading of the spaces and allow us to associate these spaces with others which are familiar to us.

A mural depicting an "alternative landscape" is located against the core wall within the three large display areas and refers to the actual landscape seen through the windows on the opposite side of the room.

Entrance to textile display

Entrance to private office

Furniture display

Sconce detail

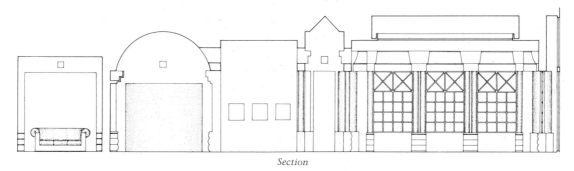

Section

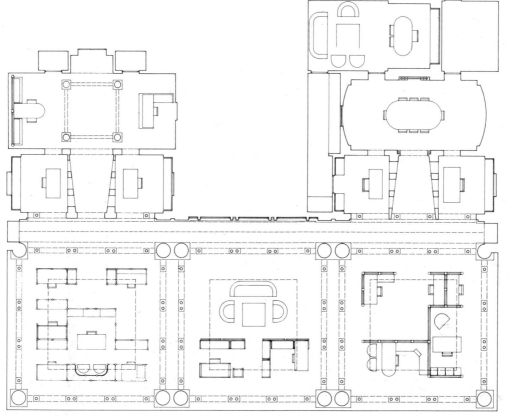

Plan

Passage soffit detail

Textile display room

Passage adjacent to furniture display rooms

1980

Yacht Club Feasibility Study
Brielle, New Jersey

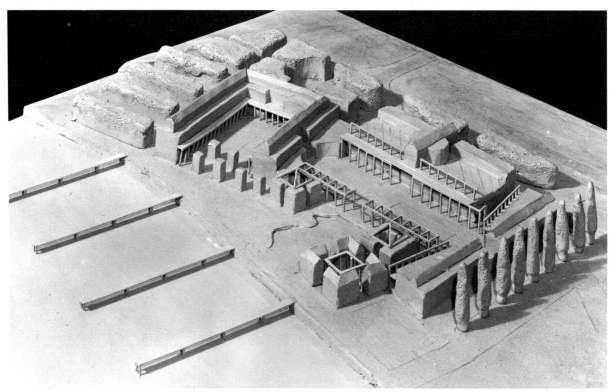

View of the study model from the harbor

The program for the yacht club includes a clubhouse with banquet halls and meeting rooms, a series of one-bedroom rental housing units, and larger condominiums to be located somewhat separate from the main complex. The clubhouse and recreational facilities have been used as the central, dominant elements in the compositions of the site. The housing blocks have been disposed to either side, forming the boundaries to the large courtyard where the pool and bar pavilion overlook the docks and the visual activities of the harbor.

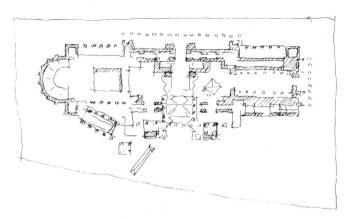
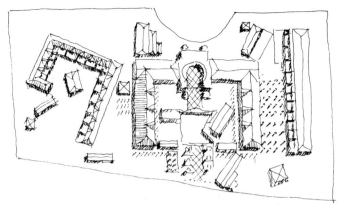
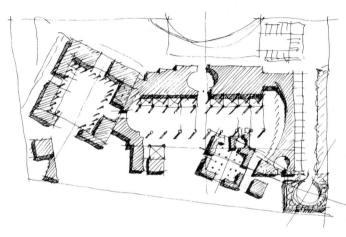
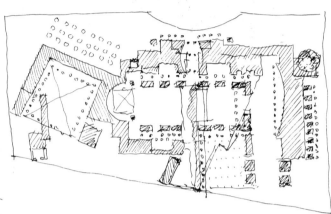
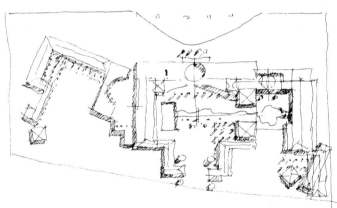
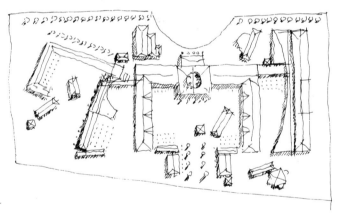

Site plan

1980

Venice Biennale
La "Strada Novissima"
Venice, Italy

Facade study

Facade study

For the 1980 Venice Biennale, twenty architects were invited to design facades for a hypothetical street erected in the Venice Arsenale. Behind each of these facades, a room was built to house an exhibition of the architect's work.

In this project, an attempt was made to describe the relationship between man himself and the architectural object as experienced in one's face to face confrontation with the plane of the facade. The tripartite arrangement of the facade into a base, *piano nobile*, and attic story corresponds to the anthropomorphic divisions of foot, body, and head. The central terra-cotta figure, by virtue of its totemic quality, not only represents us but also serves hierarchically to identify the door as the place for passage through the facade. The green columns flanking the door repeat the gesture locally and can be seen to suggest, through their polychromy, the "landscape" beyond the wall surface. Within the middle ground or *piano nobile* is located an enlarged sconce projecting from the facade. In its thrust from the facade, the sconce implies a "borrowing" of space from the street, thereby further elaborating the idea of passage from outside to inside. At the same time, the sconce acts as a balcony or raised ground plane upon which is placed an allegorical "first house."

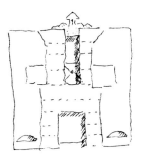

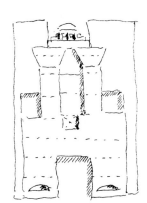

Facade and plan

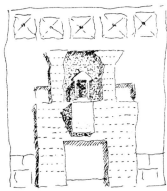

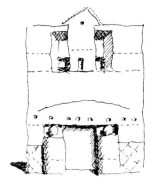

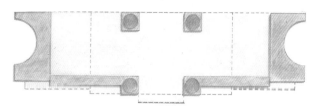

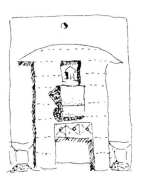

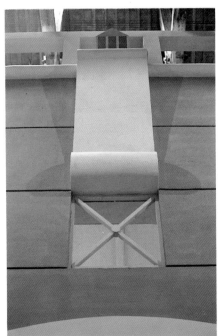

Sconce detail

Entrance detail

1980

Environmental Education Center
Liberty State Park

Jersey City, New Jersey

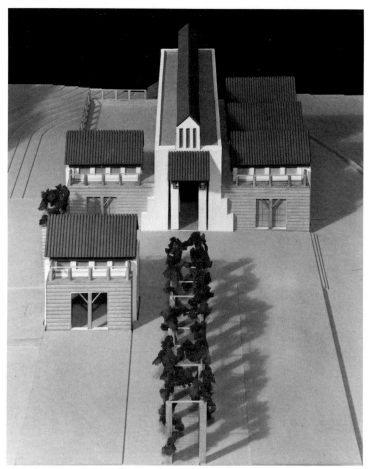

Southwest view of model toward the entrance

The Environmental Education Center is located within Liberty State Park in Jersey City, New Jersey. It is oriented with a view both to the Statue of Liberty and to the southern tip of Manhattan. The building is located on an internal road which will, in the future, connect the several facilities planned for the park.

The program for the building calls for a "wildlife interpretive center" to be used generally as a center for environmental education. Its role in the park is twofold. First, within the building, there will be exhibitions, lectures, and conferences concerning the indigenous wildlife and the environmental context of the park and the surrounding region. Second, extending from the building into the marshy landscape, there will be a path system which loops through a series of descriptive pavilions and back to the building. The building itself is organized in such a way as to suggest an equity between these two primary functions. Entering from the access road, one is given, on one side, the enclosed exhibition spaces, and on the other side, the natural outdoor exhibition.

The internal plan groups three exhibition galleries off a central entrance hall. The major themes of the center will be developed through permanent and changing exhibitions in these galleries. The galleries receive natural light through windows oriented toward New York harbor, and also through the clerestories of the light monitors above which identify the three separate areas. Also opening from the entrance hall are the public auditorium, meeting room, administrative office and exhibit preparation space.

A window located above the stage area of the auditorium provides a view beyond to a bird house, so that even from within the building, one's association with the wildlife of the park is continued. The building is clad in cedar siding and stucco, and has clay tile roofs over wooden trusses, materials which are indigenous to the Jersey shore.

Pavilion studies

Site plan

Preliminary harbor elevation

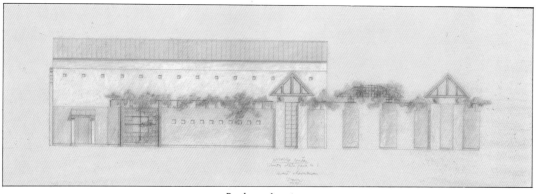

Roadway elevation

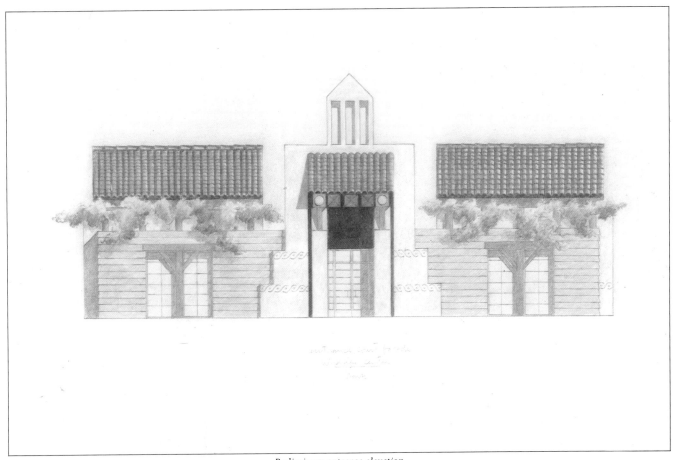

Preliminary entrance elevation

Entrance elevation

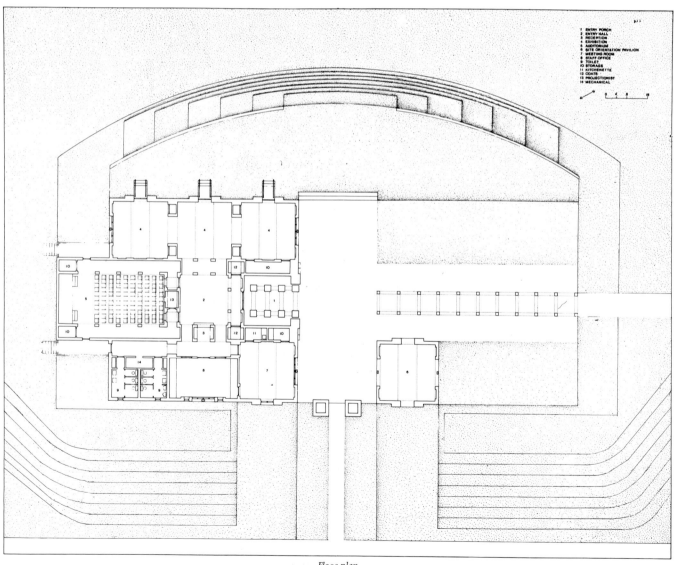

1 ENTRY PORCH
2 ENTRY HALL
3 RECEPTION
4 EXHIBITION
5 AUDITORIUM
6 SITE ORIENTATION PAVILION
7 MEETING ROOM
8 STAFF OFFICE
9 TOILET
10 STORAGE
11 KITCHENETTE
12 COATS
13 PROJECTIONIST
14 MECHANICAL

Floor plan

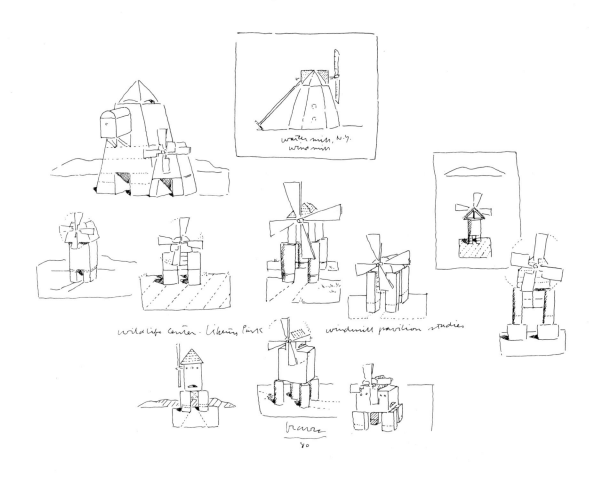

Preliminary roadway elevation

Preliminary entrance elevation

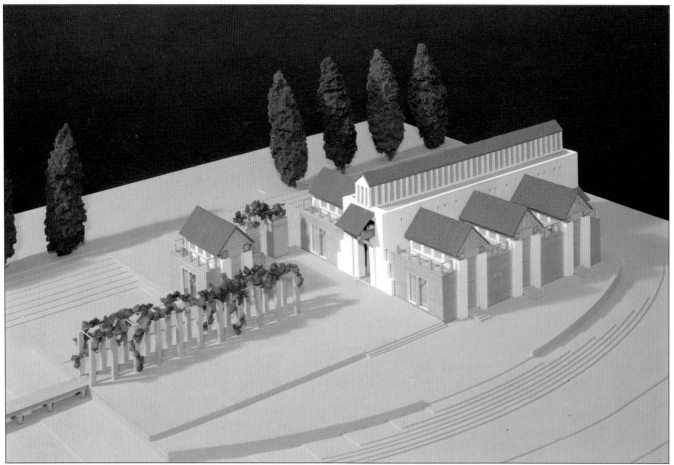

Model view from the harbor

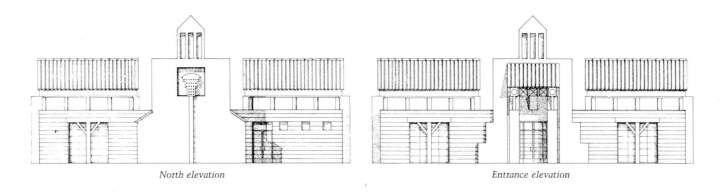

North elevation

Entrance elevation

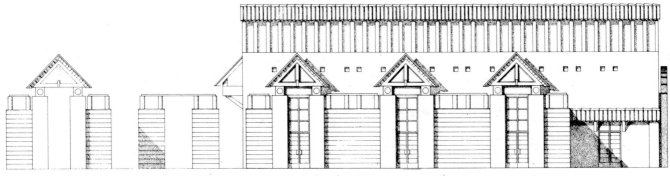

Harbor elevation

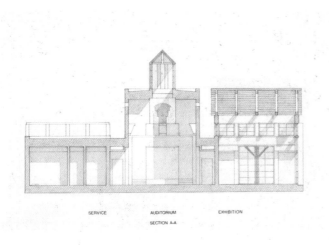

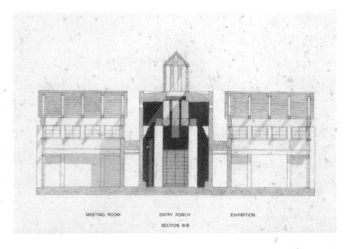

SERVICE   AUDITORIUM   EXHIBITION

SECTION A-A

MEETING ROOM   ENTRY PORCH   EXHIBITION

SECTION B-B

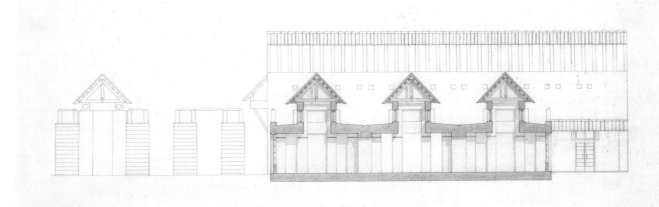

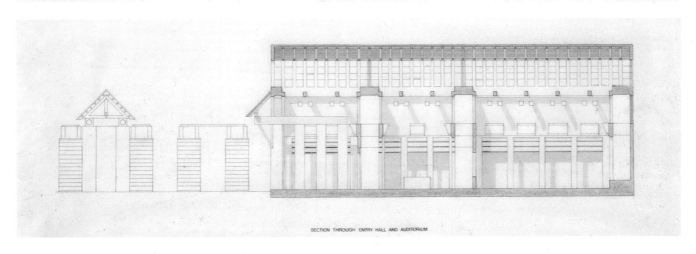

SECTION THROUGH ENTRY HALL AND AUDITORIUM

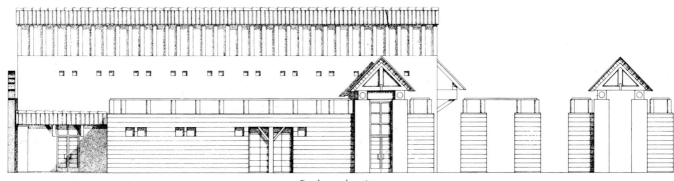

Roadway elevation

Entry court

Entry gate

1980

Apartment Building Conversion
Soho
New York, New York

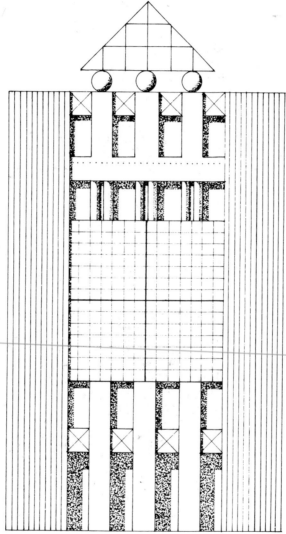

Street elevation

An existing storage warehouse in Soho is to be converted to condominium apartments. The existing building extends through the block and can therefore take advantage of the light offered from both streets. Each floor will accommodate four units, two at each street edge. The existing structure of the warehouse divides the building mid-span; that central structural division is expressed in the original building, dividing it into rather awkward left and right sides. Instead of disguising the central division of the total mass, an attempt was made to unify the building by taking advantage of this condition. An oversized "window" with decorative mullions is used to mark this division which describes both the internal plan arrangements and the original structural elements. Also, the building, which has a new floor added to its original six stories, can be read with some ambiguity: the facade expresses the divisions and character of individual apartments and at the same time can be read as a large urban house with commercial facilities on the ground floor.

Street elevation

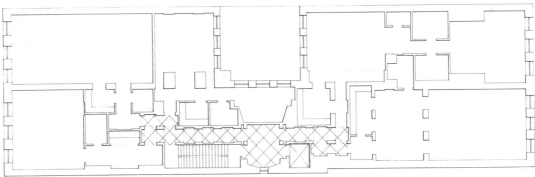

Typical floor plan

1980

Sunar Furniture Showroom
Los Angeles, California

The showroom is organized to show furniture and fabric in a variety of architectural settings. The visitor is led through a series of linked spaces which offer orientation to larger display areas beyond and which are characterized by a variety of volumetric configurations, and polychromatic and textural qualities. The display areas are designed so that an equity is established between the object in the room and the room itself. Several small and medium sized spaces have been designated for domestic furniture and small office groupings, and there are two large open spaces to accommodate Sunar's various office systems.

The fabric showroom acts as a foreground pavilion or gate to the general showroom spaces behind it. Upon entrance to the second floor of the building from the elevator, one is offered the option of entering the fabric pavilion, moving through its several rooms to the showrooms beyond, or, alternatively, of by-passing the fabric display and entering the furniture showrooms directly. The fabric pavilion is recognizable from the exterior by the use of decorative fabric swags which heighten one's awareness of fabric and decorative cloth in general.

Textile pavilion entrance

Foyer

Textile pavilion facade

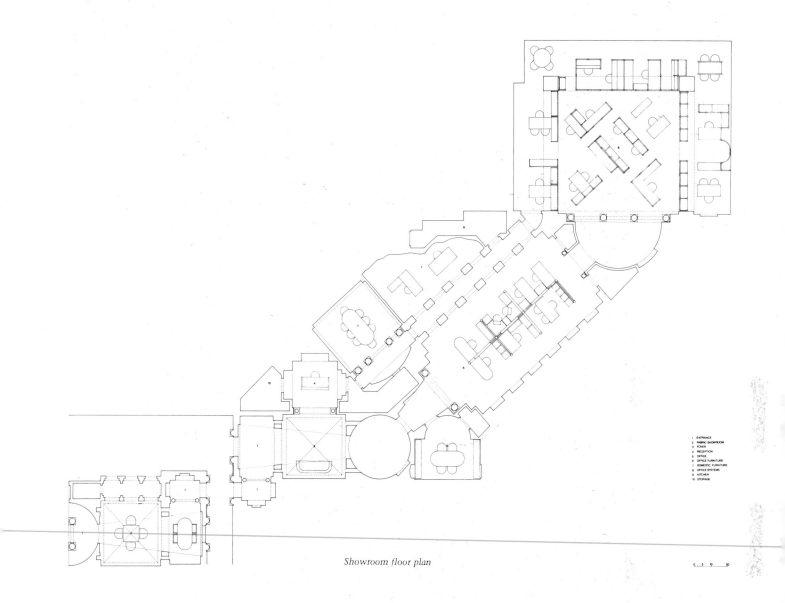

Showroom floor plan

1 ENTRANCE
2 FABRIC SHOWROOM
3 FOYER
4 RECEPTION
5 OFFICE
6 OFFICE FURNITURE
7 DOMESTIC FURNITURE
8 OFFICE SYSTEMS
9 KITCHEN
10 STORAGE

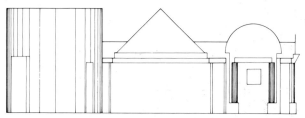

Section through library

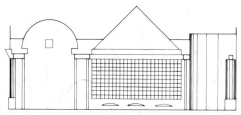

Section through library

Foyer

Fabric display

Fabric showroom exterior

1980

Tea Service

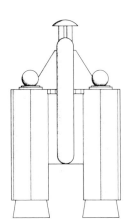 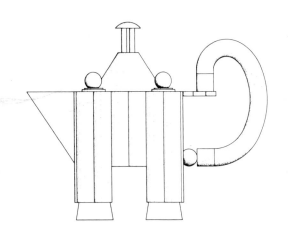 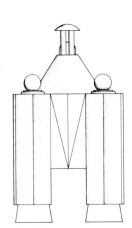

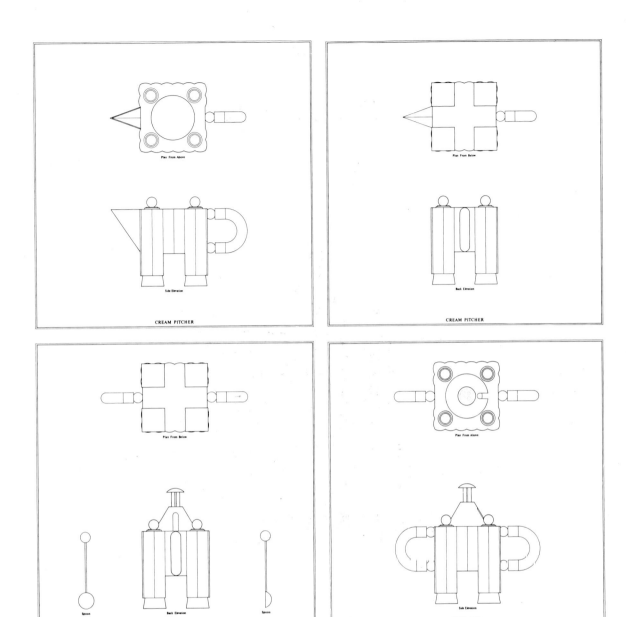

This tea service was designed as part of a series to be produced by Alessi in Milan.

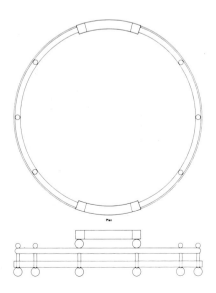

1979

Apartment Renovation
New York, New York

Library with mural

Two rooms in an existing New York apartment have been renovated, one for a family library and the other for a child's bedroom. The existing plan is organized by aisle or side entries to the library from the hall and the master bedroom. This circulation pattern has been continued and the plan of the new spaces has been developed according to this "basilican" type. The columns dividing the aisle from the main rooms, both in the library and in the bedroom, become the receptacles for the books and objects to be displayed. Thus the character of the rooms is set by both the intended uses and the preexisting circulation pattern.

The end or west axis of the child's bedroom looks to the Hudson River. Because of the similarity in plan of the two rooms, a mural depicting an "alternative landscape" has been painted on the corresponding west wall of the library in order to refer to the actual landscape beyond.

Hallway

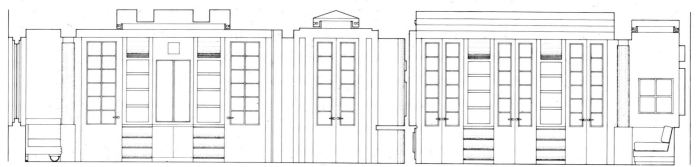

Section through playroom, child's study, and library

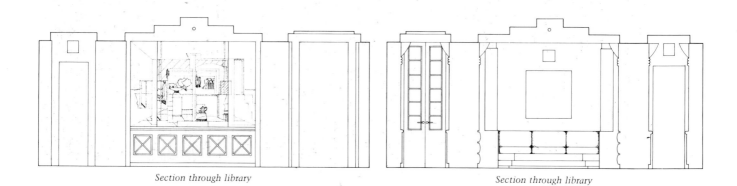

Section through library

Section through library

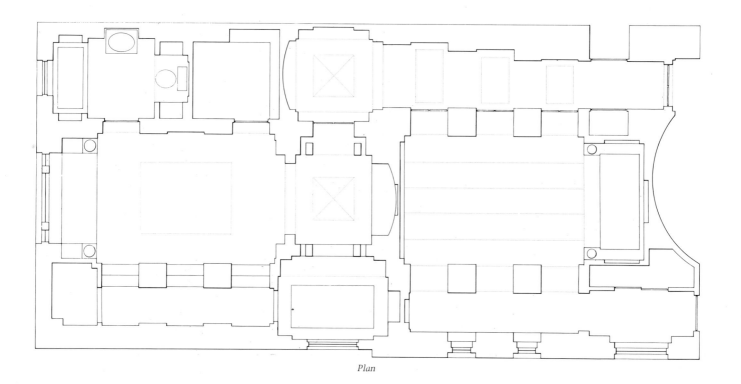

Plan

"Alternative Landscape" mural

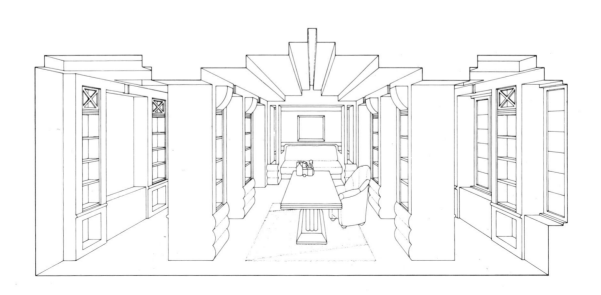

Playroom

Playroom

Bed alcove

Child's desk

Couch detail

Bed alcove

1979-1980

Exhibits and Installations

V'Soske exhibition booth ASID convention, New York 1980

Pavilion for "Michael Graves Works in the West" Exhibition at the University of Southern California, Los Angeles, 1981

Construction photograph of Sunar pavilion at the National AIA convention, Minneapolis, 1981

Metropolitan Home, Apartment hallway

1980

Public Library
San Juan Capistrano, California

View of library entrance from the street

A local ordinance in San Juan Capistrano has set guidelines for the town's architecture which require that it follow the indigenous Spanish mission style. For the library project, this has prompted an investigation of the properties of this style as a generic type. Of specific interest are the quality and variety of light in this architecture, as it was this concern which transformed the type from its Renaissance beginnings. Treatment of light is also thought to be particularly appropriate in the design of a library.

This theme is understood in the building through the use of light monitors, clerestories, and walls as filters of light. The organization of the building around a courtyard is not only appropriate because it is generic to the type but also because it allows the filtering of light from the openness at the center, to the screen of its peristyle and finally to the rooms behind. Furthermore, the courtyard serves as a place of repose for the pleasures of reading at the center of the building's organization. The court allows thematic subdivisions of the various primary internal uses required in the program without sacrificing an overall reading of unity. Quite generally, the adult section is located on one face of the courtyard, the children's wing on the second, the auditorium on the third, and garden gazebos on the fourth.

The courtyard is marked by four cypresses centering on a rather romantic stream of water which issues from the upper level of the site, organized around the auditorium forecourt pool. There is some symbolism intended in the "fall of the water" from the higher level to the courtyard "ground," as we as a society tend to make referential connections between archetypal elements in nature and our invented literature. The sustenance of the water in a physical sense is, of course, akin to the sustenance provided by material held within the library itself.

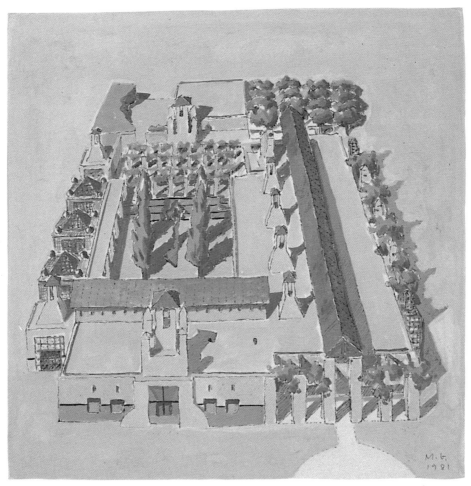

View from the south

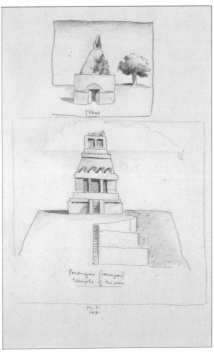

Referential sketches

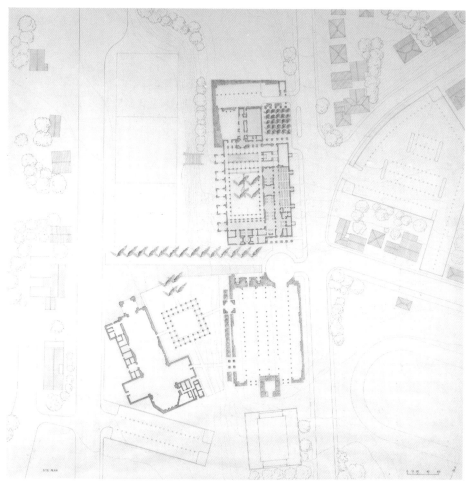

Site plan

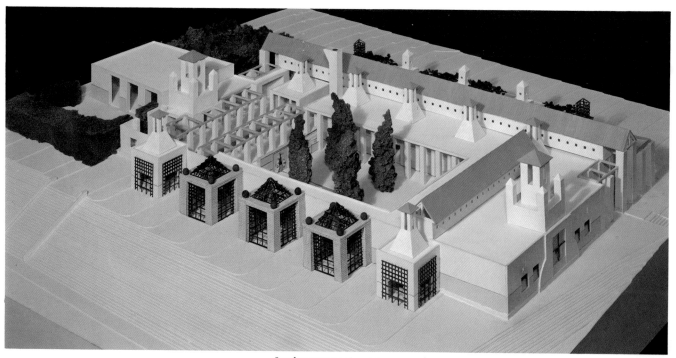

Southwest view of model

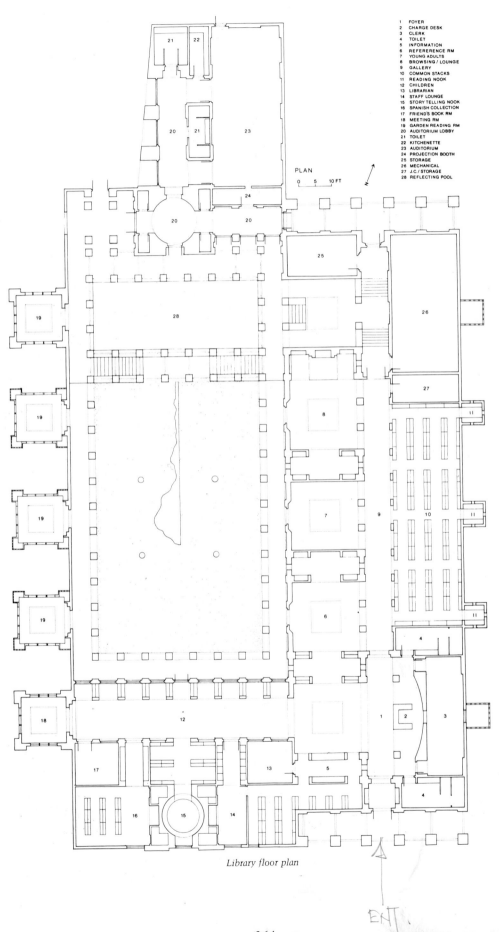

1   FOYER
2   CHARGE DESK
3   CLERK
4   TOILET
5   INFORMATION
6   REFERERENCE RM
7   YOUNG ADULTS
8   BROWSING / LOUNGE
9   GALLERY
10 COMMON STACKS
11 READING NOOK
12 CHILDREN
13 LIBRARIAN
14 STAFF LOUNGE
15 STORY TELLING NOOK
16 SPANISH COLLECTION
17 FRIEND'S BOOK RM
18 MEETING RM
19 GARDEN READING RM
20 AUDITORIUM LOBBY
21 TOILET
22 KITCHENETTE
23 AUDITORIUM
24 PROJECTION BOOTH
25 STORAGE
26 MECHANICAL
27 J.C. / STORAGE
28 REFLECTING POOL

Library floor plan

Entrance

Section through auditorium lobby, courtyard and reading rooms

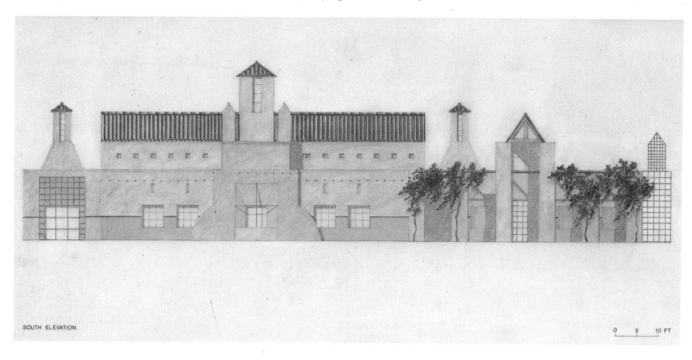

SOUTH ELEVATION

0   5   10 FT

SECTION AA

0   5   10 FT

EAST ELEVATION

0   5   10 FT

Model view of the entrance facade

Southwest view of model

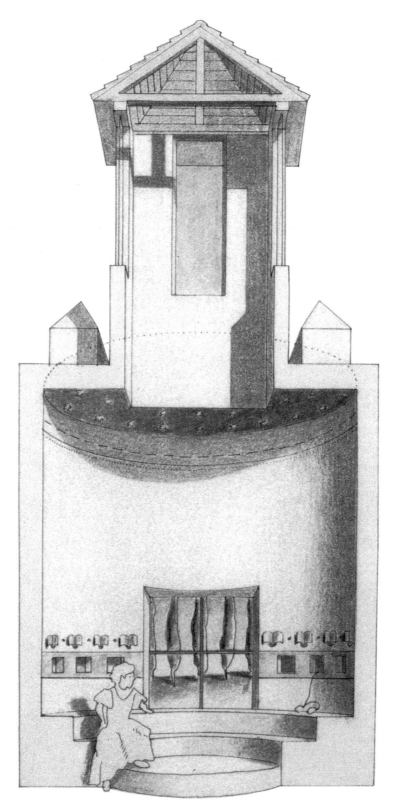

Children's reading room

1981

Bacchanal
"Artist-Architect Collaboration"
With Lennart Anderson
New York, New York

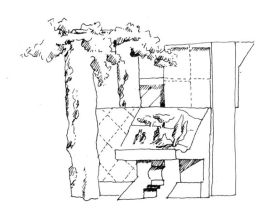

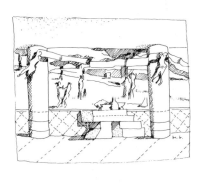

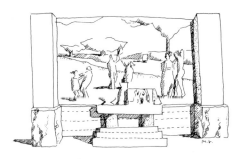

For an exhibition and publication commemorating the centennial anniversary of the Architectural League of New York, several artists and architects were commissioned to develop collaborative projects. This collaboration with the painter Lennart Anderson was based on a common interest in figurative themes and the roles of interior and exterior landscapes; it uses the theme of the bacchanal, whose elements have occurred in the work of both the artist and the architect over many years. The architect's role in this project was thought to be traditional, in providing the walls, the room, and the setting within which the painting would be placed.

"Bacchanal" installation

1981

Sunar Furniture Showroom
New York, New York

Entrance

The showroom is organized in such a way as to lead the observer through a variety of spaces from the entrance foyer through the showroom itself, with a termination at the daylight offered to the south on 56th Street. This is accomplished by a series of small rooms which offer orientation to the larger spaces containing textiles and office systems as well as domestically scaled furniture. Between each of these major elements of the Sunar collection, there is an attempt to give spatial continuity without surrendering the individual spatial enclosures of the rooms themselves. It was our intention to provide a sense of discovery through the several rooms and at the same time to offer an understanding of the whole plan. By the use of elements such as ceiling heights, surface textures, and variations in lighting, it is hoped that the observer is able to make familiar associations with places past.

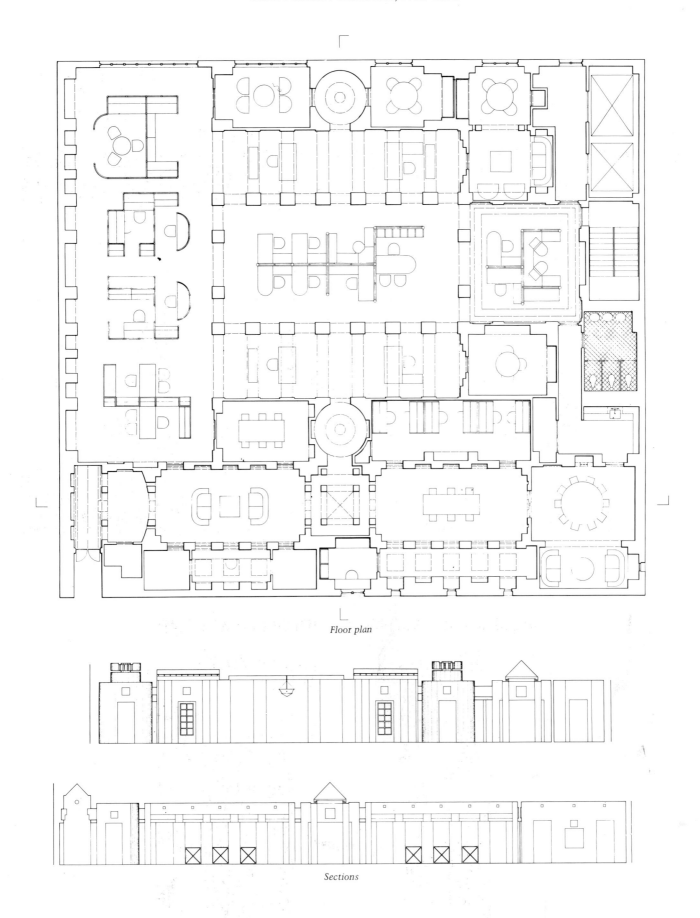

Floor plan

Sections

Textile display

View from entrance toward reception

Graves table and the textile display room

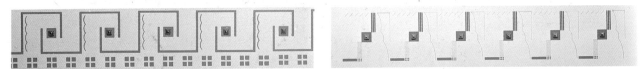

Wall stencils

Office furniture display

Vestibule to offices

Domed room, entrance to office furniture display

View from the reception area toward the entrance

View toward reception and entrance

Office furniture display

View from the reception area toward the textile display room

Reception

Dressing Table

Dressing Table for Memphis Furniture Company, Milan

It was the intention to make a piece of furniture that belongs within the existing traditions of craft, of body reference, and of symbol. Ancient furniture registered the societal station of the user inasmuch as it functioned as a generally understood symbol of culture, and it also made anthropomorphic associations. In the same way that buildings are traditionally understood to have bases or feet, bodies or hearts, and cornices or heads, a similar anthropomorphism has long been in operation in the realm of furniture. This dressing table aspires to resee the artifact as replica both of building and of man. The piece was designed for the Memphis furniture company in Milan.

1981

Cover Design

Cover design for Architectural Review Magazine

1981

Art Department and Museum
Vassar College

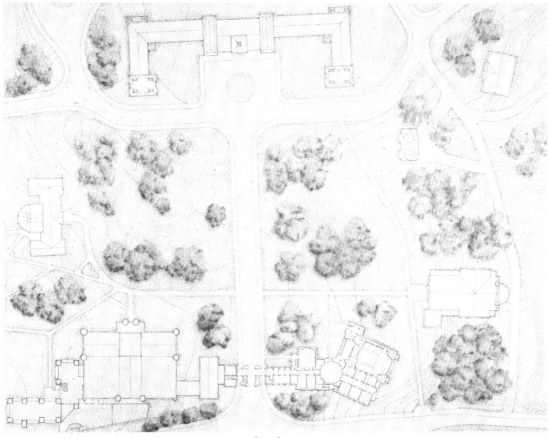

Site plan

The addition to the existing art history building will nearly double the size of their present teaching spaces. The existing building, through its carriage arch, forms the main entrance to the campus, much of which was designed in a typical collegiate Gothic style. The interior of the art history building was extensively renovated around 1940 and therefore no longer retains any trace of its original Gothic character. The project will renovate their building again and add extensively to its southern face. Besides a reorganization of the existing faculty offices, slide library, teaching spaces, and art museum, the project includes new seminar rooms, photograph study areas, gallery space, and a lecture hall. There has been an attempt to ''hinge'' the new building to the existing one by a large domed hall. This central room will be used for orientation and disbursement to both the new and the old buildings. It will also act as an anteroom for the new 600-seat auditorium. This auditorium will be used not only by the art history faculty but also to the college at large, and therefore its relationship to the central hall becomes crucial in its dual role.

The addition does not attempt to make historical allusions to the existing building but identifies archetypal elements which become a basis for the formal organization of the new wing. Though the existing building is made of Indiana limestone, the new building will, because of budget restrictions, only have stone detailing, while the major vertical surfaces will be stucco and therefore retain the sheer or taut surface quality of the original stone.

East view of model toward the entrance

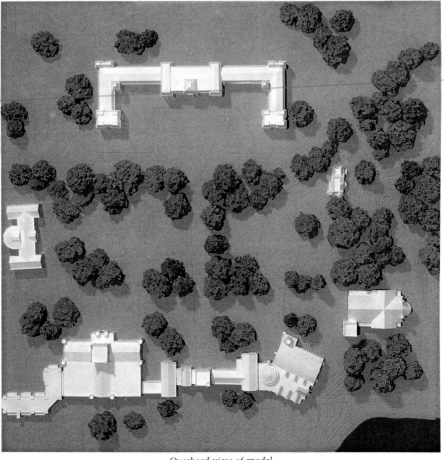

Overhead view of model

Street elevation

Entrance elevation

Street elevation study

Court elevation study

South elevation study

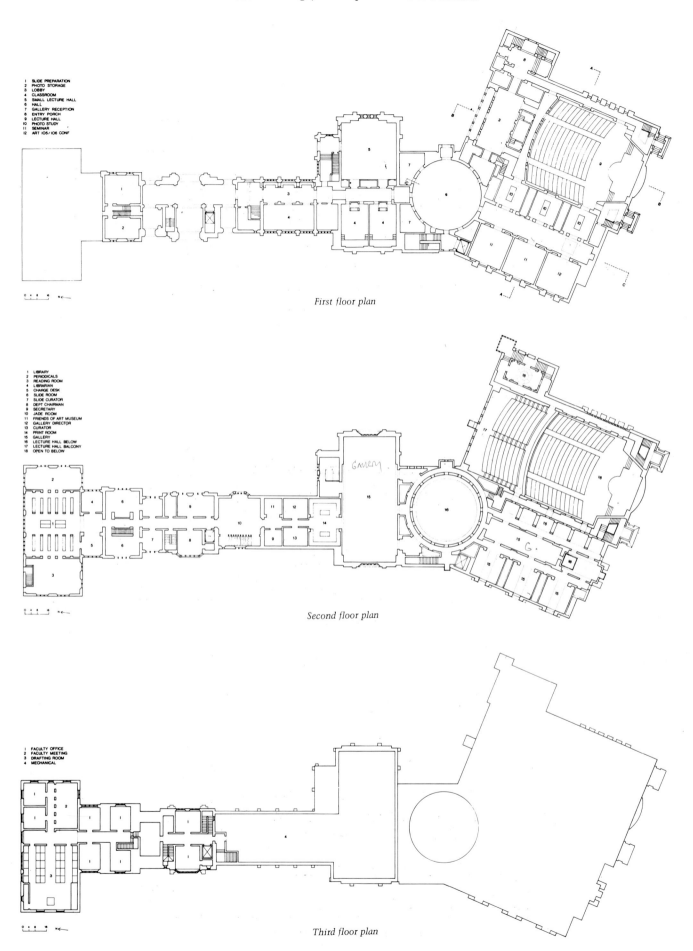

First floor plan

1 SLIDE PREPARATION
2 PHOTO STORAGE
3 LOBBY
4 CLASSROOM
5 SMALL LECTURE HALL
6 HALL
7 GALLERY RECEPTION
8 ENTRY PORCH
9 LECTURE HALL
10 PHOTO STUDY
11 SEMINAR
12 ART 105 / 106 CONF

Second floor plan

1 LIBRARY
2 PERIODICALS
3 READING ROOM
4 LIBRARIAN
5 CHARGE DESK
6 SLIDE ROOM
7 SLIDE CURATOR
8 DEPT CHAIRMAN
9 SECRETARY
10 JADE ROOM
11 FRIENDS OF ART MUSEUM
12 GALLERY DIRECTOR
13 CURATOR
14 PRINT ROOM
15 GALLERY
16 LECTURE HALL BELOW
17 LECTURE HALL BALCONY
18 OPEN TO BELOW

Third floor plan

1 FACULTY OFFICE
2 FACULTY MEETING
3 DRAFTING ROOM
4 MECHANICAL

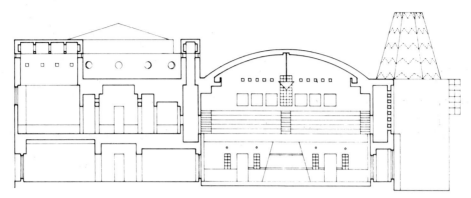

Section through lecture hall and seminar rooms

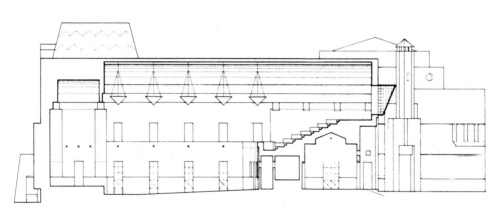

Section through lecture hall

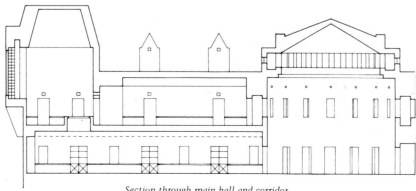

Section through main hall and corridor

East view of model

View of model from the street

South view of model

North view of model

MICHAEL GRAVES' ALLUSIVE ARCHITECTURE
The Problem of Mass

by Vincent Scully

Michael Graves' architecture more closely approximates a literary art than any other architecture one can think of in history. It has, true enough, its precursors in the sixteenth, eighteenth and nineteenth centuries, but all of them are more directly physical, less wholly allusive than itself. It depends in fact upon two words: "allusion" and "illusion". Its forms consistently allude to others and make us see what isn't there. As such it comes as close to carrying out a linguistic program as any architecture can do. More than the work of any other architect it is a conscious attempt to translate contemporary "semiotics" into architectural form —or perhaps it would be better to say that it attempts to create architecture through a semiotic method. But architecture is not only or even primarily sign and allusion; it is above all else three-dimensional mass and defined space. In one kind of balance or another with nature it creates the entire human environment, and it is experienced physically by human beings—experienced empathetically, in what might be called a pre-semiotic state of perception. That physical presence is architecture's primary meaning; upon it all associational elements, all signs, symbols, illusions and allusions are hung, and are interwoven with it. The form itself so embodies and/or signifies the whole.

Graves' problem, therefore, has been how to make a convincing architecture out of his allusions. For some time it seemed that he could perhaps do so only in drawing, at which he is a supreme master. Drawing works with the very stuff of illusion; through it, for example, plastic bodies of enormous bulk and solidity may be brought in being, as they are in Graves' preparatory sketches. Through it, especially through color—where Graves developed his own haunting hues—the final project may take on a peculiarly evocative quality, suggestive of depths of meaning not easy to classify, rich in allusion.

Translated into building, however, such pictorial effects tend, by definition, to cling to the surface, as if they might lose their allusive quality if they were transformed into mass. Yet Graves' sources in classical architecture are massive ones, and in his preparatory sketches he has shown for some time that he is able to endow those masses with a

This essay tries to treat the development of Graves' more recent projects and buildings as a chronological sequence of design, but it does not deal with all his architectural work, with his mural paintings, or perhaps enough with his color, which is in any event amply documented in this volume. Whatever I have set down owes an enormous debt to Peter Arnell, without whose unselfish help and close association with Graves' architecture over many years it could hardly have been written at this time. I am also grateful to Karen Vogel Wheeler and to Michael Graves himself.

new, rather eerie life. Has he now finally begun to translate that quality into definitive drawings and, most of all, into built forms? Portland stands as the early phase of any answer, indicating that it can perhaps be done, may already have been accomplished there. But the questions involved are complex and contradictory ones. They are important enough for architecture as an art to deserve consideration at some length and in relation to the structure of Graves' work as a whole. The work itself has already produced objects of such beauty that its development can be pursued with pleasure and respect as well.

To a New Englander, Princeton has a Southern air, heavy and still. On the fashionable west side of town the houses are set far back from the street on richly landscaped lots. They are many in number and normally large in size, and they all carry themselves like "mansions", as few New England houses do. Many more of them than in New England are built of brick or masonry or have stuccoed walls. There is a somnolence, supremely self-engrossed and satisfied. On the east the houses are smaller, but the general character is much the same. The residential blocks are equally leafy and well grown up; the streets are heavily shaded. Michael Graves lives in a converted warehouse which is set in the middle of one of the blocks, behind the other houses and well away from the street, in a situation very rare in American urbanism. The building itself was built by Italian workmen in the 1920's, when they were constructing Princeton's Gothic campus nearby. It is of stuccoed brick with a short overhang and small, deep-set, cross-mullioned windows. It has a decidedly Tuscan air. A later addition, shaping a courtyard, was left unstuccoed at the request of the neighbors, who have in any case always regarded this intrusive building with distaste, and its brick surface is thickly covered with ivy, also at their request. Inside, Graves' renovations develop slowly; the effect in part recalls that often found in Italy, where modern occupants may camp in the shell of a noble, partly ruined villa with exposed structure and naked walls. Graves has surfaced his driveway and courtyard with light-colored crushed stone, and has begun to lay out a high-hedged garden. Shielded by trees from the surrounding houses out of contact with the street, the house does in fact suggest the ambience of a villa in Italy, rather a rustic example on a white dusty road south of Florence, where the signori lunch al fresco under the thin shade of an arbor through the midday hours. In any case, the effect is wholly Mediterranean; one could hardly be farther from the United States.

Graves' Benacerraf House, of 1969, his first constructed work in Princeton, has exactly these qualities: set in the middle of a block, wholly European in inspiration, totally without respect for its immediate architectural context. The project involved the remodelling of an Anglo-American "free-style" house of about 1900. The other houses on the block are of similar character, and the only part of Graves' renovation which is visible on the exterior is projected like a garden pavilion from the rear of its house into the central space of the block as a whole, which is warmly defined by the brown stucco and dark trim of the preexisting buildings. Among these Graves' confection explodes like a bomb, forever disturbing their quiet. The effect is intended, and it may perhaps be seen as a direct result of Graves' middle-western background and his architectural training at Harvard and the American Academy in Rome. It is a young man's polemic, highly "aesthetic" and theoretical, against his immediate surroundings, against—we recall Sinclair Lewis—Main Street. It snubs the actual environment in order to quote esoteric fragments of Rietveld and Le Corbusier and to gesture to "pure" nature as hedge, branch, and cloud. The resultant forms are forensic and theatrical, and unlike their older neighbors they have weathered rather badly.

In these ways Graves' Benacerraf addition belongs to the International Style, or rather represents that special and rather nostalgic revival of the early days of the International Style which took place in the sixties and is best associated with the so-called New York Five of Eisenman, Graves, Gwathmey, Hejduk, and Meier. One characteristic of the revival is that its forms are less purely volumetric than those of the earlier work. Their attempt to expound certain linguistic and structuralist theories intervenes to complicate architecture's fundamental spatial function and sometimes to contravene it. Hence Graves' complex structure does not in fact release the interior spaces of its house. Instead, its articulations smother them. The curving wall confines and reduces the interior volume just at the point where it promises expansion to the garden, and the staircase is set down directly athwart the releasing line of sight. Much the same is true of the Claghorn addition, of 1974, which is also in the rear of a more or less vernacular Shingle-Style house. By this time, though, a change is beginning to be apparent in Graves' work. He has said that he began to wish to say more than could be done with bare surfaces. So he overspread his International Style articulations of frame and plane with a layered cladding of varying colors, intended to refer, along with nature, not to the heroes of the modern movement but to the old house itself—or rather, an important point, to what Graves refers to as "its own classical sources". He thus persists in refusing to honor the American vernacular, but skirts the issue and achieves something close to the necessary connection with it by pulling out of or projecting upon it that element he does value: the classical tradition of form. That tradition includes the classical garden. So pediments are referred to in the layering, and pergolas as well. Nature, as if classically weighed in some symbolic and mythic way beyond the actual suburban situation, is alluded to by colors: dark earth, deep green, blue sky. It seems a curious alchemy, but it stems from Graves' own deep determination to create forms which deal with what he regards as architecture's symbolic functions in some primal and archetypal way, one which will therefore recognize only the grandest and most enduring of human traditions. So it is classicism, with its columns and its snakes, its rustic arbors and its rusticated palace walls, whose ancient grip shakes him out of the International Style but leaves him—indeed gives him—his beloved Mediterranean, the setting of his directing fantasy, and so sets him free as an artist.

We cannot help but ask what caused this new focus, what suddenly (or so it appears) made classicism seem to Graves to be available for his use? His sketchbooks show that the shift was not in fact overnight, and that he sat in juries during 1975 at Princeton, Harvard, and Yale sketching furiously away, hollowing out masses of masonry or garden hedges, beginning, at least in these quick sketches, to carve forms out of solids like Leonardo in his notebooks and Bramante among St. Peter's piers. But something changed him. Can contact with Leon Krier, whose stern devotion to rigorously classical and vernacular forms had just played a measurable part in setting James Stirling on his mature way, have played a role here? Krier was teaching in Princeton during the critical year or two. Perhaps increased contact with the architects of the renewed Shingle-Style and their stylistic allusions played some complementary part. Robert Venturi's application of evocative moldings to the surface of his family's house of 1962-64 comes especially to mind. And even more systematically than Venturi, who regards it as "too easy", Graves was never to employ classical forms in a directly recognizable guise. In that sense he remains, like Venturi, a "modern" architect, seeking equivalents, not simulacra. So a tension arises, perhaps a creative one. Unlike the typical Late-Modern architect, who sought in each project to reinvent the wheel, Graves seeks to create a new, or alternative, classical vocabulary. Is it a self-defeating aim, or an essential one? Whatever the case, by 1975 Graves was ready. The Crooks project, of 1975-76, was the first to show his power. Now it is house and garden together: the house an International Style box turning before our eyes into a palazzo block with a courtyard, the garden a clearing hollowed out of solid greenery. The two begin to respond to each other in numerous ways, always in metamorphosis through drawing after drawing. The house thickens, solidifies, but begins to break down on the surface—to be decorated, in fact. And the closer it comes to final form the more pictorial, rather than sculpturally massive, it becomes. There is a curious duality, which Alan Colquhoun, in a brilliant essay, has seen as essential to Graves' concept of architecture as complex "representation" rather than, we might say, the simple construction of a "durable" reality. There are clearly problems in this, since architecture is durable reality. The answer to the problem might be said to lie in the recognition of the fact that architecture communicates physically as well as through association. Both ways of communication involve signs, but the physical are empathetically, rather than associationally, perceived. Graves, though, is involved with the associational esthetic of his linguistically oriented colleagues, and this itself acts toward keeping his sign system pictorial and representational in the face of other influences, such as that from classicism itself, which would tend to push it toward physical bulk. The continuing hold of what might be called International Style cubism on his pictorial imagination also plays a part. Hence the duality: rustication of a sort develops, but it is made to drift like cloud across the surfaces of house, courtyard wall, and garage in a complex set of figures of such low relief that they seem to be primarily painting. They create a composition much like those of Graves' earlier murals, especially that in the early Hanselmann House of 1967. It is all scenographics unashamed, all theater. The house itself seems pulled to gesture toward the courtyard, its corners crumbling under the strain, while the axes of the garden start to shoot out radially like the first, still uneven rays of a classical star. In the garden's shapes one is reminded not only of the French seventeenth century but also, more immediately, of Gertrude Jekyll's masses of greenery advancing on Lutyens' houses and thrust back by them. But in Graves' project the garden is much more massive than the building—because there he is not held by his International Style/linguistic esthetic. Inside the house, however, rooms begin to take shape.

South view of model

North view of model

by Vincent Scully

Graves himself is very clear about this as an important break-through in his design. The International Style was deter-mined, apparently as part of its process, to destroy the con-cept of "room". The idea goes farther back, even to Wright: it was all to be one democratic flow. Hence a return to the concept of a sequence of separate room shapes, defined one from the other in character and function, but most of all per-ceived as special symbolic places, is a new and essential thought, and one both spatial in essence and suggestive of sculptural embellishment. Rooms are no longer to be sim-ply suggested as areas of flowing space in the International Style manner, but are to be formed as discrete classical vol-umes, heavily shaped by solid wall masses and menaced by enormous fireplace breasts, protean in form. A newly vigor-ous architecture begins to develop, alive in space and sculp-tural action as well. New furniture must therefore take shape, evocative of traditional forms and at once heavier, more volumetric, and more active than that of the Interna-tional Style, and from this time onward furniture sketches abound in Graves' notebooks.

While all this was being studied, Graves entered a bril-liant proposal in a competition for high-rise housing in Trenton. Here he was already able to put classical lessons to use in an intractable contemporary program. He interwove several layers of rhythm into the skeletal facade and increased its solidity, while at the same time causing the mass as a whole to inflect toward the garden. That inflection recalls the similar movement in Venturi's building for the Visiting Nurse Association in Ambler, Pennsylvania, of 1961. The influence of that building has been generously acknowl-edged by Graves. Its use of applied decoration to build up the scale of its windows had probably already affected the decoration of his surfaces. He was still to exploit and to carry much further the deep classical drama of entrance to which its own primitively arched and diagonally-beamed entrance-way ultimately referred.

So the modest Schulman addition which came along at this moment in Graves' work is very different from the ear-lier ones. It now deploys laterally across the facade of the existing house, setting up a more monumental front door on the way, and then extends beyond it, increasing in scale at each stage of its progress until the clapboards of its garden wall become enormous, like colossal masonry. The whole is pure surface, and surface illusion, but everything becomes bigger and grander, with very economical means, while the new living room is a clear volume of space dominated by a rusticated fireplace, drawn back like a looming curtain of comparatively gigantic scale: but still a curtain, not a mass. Toward the garden the new surface of the house is treated as a lattice, visually weightless in comparison to the monu-mentally evocative entrance facade.

It was at this moment that Graves acquired his Tuscan farmhouse in the center of the block. He was ready for this, too, and it might be argued that its availability set the seal of conviction on his fantasy world. He painted large-scale il-lusionistic rustication at the head of its driveway and on its chimney mass and prepared a deep open volume of space as a new entrance for it. That void hollowed out of the building joined the murals in creating a powerfully architectural ef-fect. The paintings themselves are outscaled versions of what used to be called the First Pompeiian Style, a trompe l'oeil rendering of masonry blocks. In this they contrast with most of the Graves' celebrated murals on interior walls—which tend to recall the Third and Fourth Styles, with delicately scaled theatrical columns, swags, drapery and spatial illusions of the type Vitruvius condemned.* At

the Princeton warehouse the effect is one very appropriate to an exterior, and it suggests experiments in modes of wall articulation as purely optical forms that Graves was to use in other buildings. Inside, the space was left largely open, always clearly shaped by the structural frame, with a long kitchen, a sitting group rising two stories to a skylight, and so on. Art deco ziggurat shapes in tile, already in evidence in the sketches for the Crooks Project, anchor the splendid bathrooms, set like Neronic visions in the raw, unfinished walls. Stepped partitions, suggestive of Amerindian origi-nals, climb up and down within the voids of the frame, while upside-down keyhole windows, the reverse of those once used by Kahn in his "ruins", now fill out the old small windows of the warehouse in response to the requirements of the building code. Skylights flood one bay or another. A living room of two stories has been blocked out but is not yet finished. It employs cylindrical metal columns on high bases reminiscent of those in Labrouste's Bibliotheque Ste. Genevieve and indeed of all nineteenth-century Gothic-Revival "colonettes en delit". Glass block finds its place in new fenestration which seeks to respect the pictorial con-tinuity of the wall. From the key figure of a herm set in the central bay, the whole ambient seems to drift upward through two stories in reversed ziggurats of cloud. It is the garden dream, and the sketches for the garden in particular have moved boldly out to the conquest of the classic realm. They are, once again, more solidly massive than those relating to the house. One sketch shows an exaggerated perspective in the manner of Le Notre, apparently carved out of solid evergreen, to which, on a cross axis, a kind of nymphaeum or bosquet is connected. The whole was to be entered from the gravel court through a primitively squat, four-piered pergola structure which recalls those of Krier. This is the secret world: the giants in the garden, Berenson in his villa, the Anglo-Saxon dream of Italy, "where angels fear to tread". One cannot help but think of David Coffin's studies of Italian gardens, and of his courses at Princeton which Graves attended and to which, so he says, all the peo-ple in his office now invariably go. But, as noted above, there is something here which is French as well. The small gardens of Le Notre, like that of "Sylvie" at Chantilly, or for Bossuet at Meaux, come to mind. Small spaces, big shapes, forced perspectives, magic scale: nothing quite like it in Italy.

Still, it is Italy which holds Graves' fancy, and it is the villas of Italy which his next important project, the Plocek House, now under construction in Warren Township, New Jersey, most immediately recalls—especially Raphael's Villa Madama high on its massive platform, unfinished, a hollowed-out cavern pulling nature into it from one side. Vignola's Caprarola is also suggested: an enormous, rusti-cated mass looming on the side of a hill, with a cylindrical courtyard within it and a garden higher up the mountain behind. Finally, there is Palladio's Villa Barbaro at Maser, where a grotto stands between the rear of the villa and the hill, in a location occupied in the Plocek project by a keystone study-shrine. Graves himself refers to the Giar-dino dell' Arcadia in Rome with its cross axis, central circle, and funnelled side entrance, and asserts that the plan of the Plocek House is directly derived from this. He shows us that relationship among what he calls his "Referential Sketches," and he tells us that such drawings are his

*One of the most recent of these, that for the Sunar showroom in New York, now culminates the long entrance vista of that rather lush interior with a double illusion, a comment on furniture and space.

"Memory," from which all of his projects derive. It is interesting that Aldo Rossi says the same thing in his *Scientific Autobiography of My Work*. This represents a recognition by both architects that their forms come from somewhere other than from flow diagrams, that indeed they come from other forms. They come in fact from whatever forms the architect has seen and "remembered". The more polemical of the International Style architects, especially of the Bauhaus school, which particularly hoped to throw out the past, hated this view of creative activity, but the record left by the most successfully "creative" of recent architects, if we may employ such an unsympathetic term, would lead us to believe that it is a true one. Louis I. Kahn's concept of Forms in the mind (which recalls Henri Focillon's similar perception of 1934*) seems related to this fundamental idea. For Graves, as for Rossi, memory is shaped by drawing; Graves' "referential sketches" are of the forms he has seen. These lead, he tells us, to the "preparatory studies" for his own work, and finally to the "definitive drawings" of his projects. So his incomparable sketchbooks, which suggest those of Le Corbusier but are much more focused upon the constant reworking both of references and of new studies than Le Corbusier's were, richly record his process of design. That process is entirely one of drawing, which Graves calls "tangible speculation". It is marvelous to leaf through these books and to watch the mind and the hand at work together, teaching each other, seeking out manifold ways to the light. There is no "solution," as in the thoughtless jargon of run-of-the-mill modernism, only a constantly unfolding process of life. What preexists slowly merges into what will become; the intensity and complexity of the action are enormous. The architect clearly never stops looking, never stops thinking; he is a transmitter of forces flowing through him from past to future, from the tangible existing to the tangible to come. Precisely for that reason it is not a hermetic process, like the fevered drawings of some late International Style architects, which feed on themselves and narcotize the mind. It deals with what is; to put it bluntly it is open to history, to the physical embodiments of human culture, and is therefore part of a civilizing process, is alike the record of history and its vehicle.

History clearly moves from model to model. We build the present on what we have isolated from the past. For Graves, as we have said, the model is the classical past, at this time specifically the Italian Renaissance. So the Plocek House is an Italian villa of almost overwhelming mass—at least in Graves' "preparatory studies" for it. All of these sketches work on the problem of digging into that mass, eating it away, hollowing it out. The stuff of creation is a solid which the pencil excavates. Finally the heavily rusticated block builds up. Yet, once again, the "definitive drawings" are much less massive than the studies. It becomes an affair of flat surface layers like stage flats, acting by their colors to suggest a somber weight in purely optical terms. Theoretically, with such a mass the major human act would be of entrance. One cannot slide in around a weightless plane. One must seem to perforate it. It opens grudgingly and seeks, at the same time, to close up the doorway again. Indeed, it compresses and fractures itself trying to squeeze down on the opening, but as one passes underneath the unstable mass it flourishes its lavish insignia in majestic greeting

overhead. Out of some sequence of actions like this the great rusticated entrances of Giulio Romano, Serlio, Palladio, and their Mannerist and Baroque descendants took form. Their rustication at once threatens and welcomes; the pediments display and are themselves the noble insignia. Beyond all else the keystone is the compelling fact; it most compresses and expands. It is also the most intensely structural fact, and at the same time the most ambiguous one: it holds the entrance together by pushing it apart. For these reasons it seems to embody the most primitive power, and from his earliest studies for the Plocek House that power in the keystone has obsessed Graves. It has become his major motif. But in the Plocek scheme it dominates by its absence. Where it would be weighing down upon the doorway there is only a void. The weight is not there. Only after penetrating the house will one discover that the keystone has been built up at gigantic scale as a separate building behind it: the study-shrine referred to earlier. It is not included in the present campaign of construction, but the owner promises that he will eventually build it without fail. So discovered, its enormous, disquietingly shaped mass will theoretically be transported by the memory of the viewer to its "proper" location, where it should come crashing down upon the doorway, filling its place and bringing its weight to bear upon the thick, cylindrical columns. At least that is the way Graves' definitive drawings showed the columns, but he has decided to build them flat, with rusticated bases, drawn more simply into the general rusticated pattern of the lower zone of the facade and so less evocative of the keystone's missing weight.

The original conception of the Plocek House, however, specifically recalls Frank Furness' Provident Life and Trust Company of 1879. There a great mass at the top compresses the facade as if it had been dropped from above, fracturing the door and window casings and driving the short, shiny columns like pistons into their casings. How American the design is in both instances. Each takes a European motif, blows it up in scale and, as it were, builds a whole building out of it, physically dramatizng that act as one fraught with awful danger. Viollet-le-duc's entrance pavilion at Pierrefonds served as the model for Furness; for Graves it is the family, indeed the savage race, of keystones as a whole. But, once again, Graves' facade is not in fact physically compressive, like Furness'. It remains all on the surface: pictorial, scenographic. Will it lack essential force—or tellingly allude to that lack? If this is seen as a problem in Graves' work, and one might argue that question in the affirmative, we should then remind ourselves that Furness himself began in a decidedly pictorial way. The facade of the Pennsylvania Academy of Fine Arts of 1872 is largely, though not entirely, a matter of colored planes, only suggestive of articulation and compression. Indeed, the rustication of its base story is treated so as to look more like painted plaster or even papier mache imitating stone than like stone itself. Later, as in the Provident Trust, the articulation, though kept to a restricted set of planes, becomes empathetically massive, structurally evocative of compressive force. Can Graves be said to stand at the earlier stage? Is it intrinsic to the vitality of his work to move on to the second?

Inside the Plocek House, in any event, some sense of physical presence will always be at work. Entrance, through the deep grotto behind the columns of the front or between the wonderful, columned, diagonal cliffs at the side, leads eventually to the central stairway, which winds as a narrow castle stair around a walled shaft in the center. Above it all is a great circular skylight, but that will be masked by an enormous capital at rotunda size stretching upward and outward

*Henry Focillon, *La Vie des Formes*,, Paris, 1934; trans. by C. B. Hogan and G. Kubler, *The Life of Forms in Art*, New Haven, 1942, Chapter IV, "Forms in the Realm of the Mind."

Frank Furness. 409 Chestnut Street. Main facade. c. 1885. Photograph by Tremaine's Architectural Photographers. Courtesy Historical Society of Pennsylvania, Philadelphis. Penrose Collection.

Pennsylvania Academy of the Fine Arts. Broad Street elevation, by Furness and Hewitt. 1873 Ink and wash on paper. Pennsylvania Academy of the Fine Arts. Philadelphia.

from the circular ring which caps the rectangular top of the closed stairwell. The capital will be coffered like a Roman vault, and some coffers will be open to let light through, but the effect may well be that of a colossal column taking up the space in the middle of the house. This recalls the physical mass of the colonial fireplaces of New England which occupy the center of their building, but Graves consciously exploits that condition to create a looming sculptural figure, in which Kahn's gigantic stairway cylinder in the hall of his British Art Center at Yale is partly recalled. From the living room of the Plocek House that figure will be especially imminent. The room is really a living hall, embedded in the body of the house, two stories high, lighted primarily from above, giving the effect of a perfect cube. Opposite its fireplace wall—where will rise up another archaic fireplace mass at the scale of Viollet-le-duc's for Pierrefonds or, even more, Furness' for the Library of the University of Pennsylvania—a balustraded gallery is intended to open onto the room at the upper level, and through it the giant capital will be seen. The effect will be of a three-dimensional projection of one of Graves' murals, here perhaps a rather Second Style example, like one of the panels from Boscoreale in the Metropolitan Museum of Art. The sculptural shape of the capital will be set back on axis within its own, as if illusionistic, volume of space behind the framing columns and the Roman balustrades.

In this way all the major experiences of the house, from entrance, to living room, to garden, will be directed by empathetic or associational reactions to aggressive physical presences. Environmental space is thus everywhere challenged by sculptural action. Whatever question may exist regarding the actual feeling of mass that the house may give there can be no doubt about its challenge to space, taking footing as it does high on its awkward hill slope with a vast view, primarily of sky, opening before it. The rusticated wall that acts as its visual base curves out into the sky like a bastion to support a monumental pergola. The whole effect is of a fortification, indeed of the hubris of man. Here one feels another kind of threat, that of Olympian retribution. The building is Titanic, an Enceladus threatening Zeus, precisely because it is so much of the earth: mountainous in mass, or suggestive of that condition, and apparently constructed of enormous blocks of stone. The latter are, however, purely visual and symbolic. Graves says that he would have been delighted to make them real, but even this budget would have rebelled at that, and one wonders, too, whether the contradictory allusiveness of the whole, probably central to its web of meanings, would not have been reduced thereby. At present, the surface is of stucco spread over plywood sheathing and marked out with a plastic grid to simulate large-scale masonry. The use of stucco itself is not untraditional; though it is employed much less in America than in Europe it does have some vernacular use in Princeton, as we noted earlier. It also served Frank Lloyd Wright as a major surface covering for his early wood frame houses and has worn very well. With stucco, sometimes latticed, and, where appropriate, with tile, Graves can create all the symbolic effects of masonry mass and large scale that, so far, he seems to want, and with it he answers those of us who worried about the permanence of his surface effects. They will require upkeep right enough, but not nearly so much as, for example, those of the canonical International Style.

Graves' symbolic colors, as we have seen, are an integral part of the somber and earthy atmosphere: here dark terracotta below in the rusticated courses and pale mauve above. Graves does in fact intend these colors to represent forces rising from heavier to lighter, and they are thus exactly the opposite in mood and meaning from the primary heraldries that the International Style preferred. They are also curiously hesitant, soft, and rather sorrowful in character. They help create a feeling of nostalgia, and tend to suggest age and ruin, and the far wall of the terrace of the Plocek House will in fact be "ruined" away in ragged steps. As in some of Palladio's villas, all this sounds a note of Mannerist melancholy in the face of nature, a mood which was thereafter to remain a constant undercurrent in Italian villa and garden design until it was transmuted into the sublime sorrows and terrors of the Romantic movement. In 1981 those terrors and sorrows assume another kind of reality in the rusticated body of a house like this. So agonized is the general condition of humanity not twenty miles away, so appalling its physical environment, that the very physical power, even brutality, that is suggested by this palatial mass seems to embody a frighteningly provocative stance. We begin to see the lightness, thinness, and bareness of the early days of the International Style as representing an apotropaic act, one which disowns responsibility for being rich. Economic conditions have not fundamentally changed since that time, so that one cannot help but wonder which stance is the more appropriate one—if such questions have any meaning in terms of the super-rational premises, processes, and effects of art. Surely Graves, like his friend Robert Stern, would be delighted to design low-cost housing, if society's priorities were saner and such programs were available to him. Should the architect then not build at all, as Leon Krier has not done? It is hard to see how such self denial can in fact help the situation; if the architect can make good architecture by building—Krier says he can't, Graves thinks he does—it may be his fundamental cultural responsibility to do so. Whatever the case, Graves in his buildings, as here, is communicating feelings of profound loss no less than of possession, of deep cultural fatigue as well as of power. His building is a poetic evocation. It is not really aggressive, not active like those of Furness, but reflective, deathly, elegiac. It is functioning, without question, in the territory of art, where no meaning is single and where the tragic structure of the fundamental human condition probably takes precedence over, indeed overwhelms, other considerations.

Such considerations, nevertheless, were not absent in the case of another of Graves' most important projects, that for a doctor's residence in New Jersey. Here the client apparently became embarrassed by the grandeur of the house as it was published in drawing and model before construction and so eventually withdrew from the project. This was sad because the building was clearly a consummate work of art. Its flat site encouraged greater suppleness and a freer extension along the horizontal plane than that possible in the Plocek House. Its program also required multiple garages so that wings and courtyards developed naturally, pushing out to the landscape and drawing it through the house, whose marvelous piers and wall masses promised, in plan, a monumental passage of spaces from court to court. The connection of the wings with the house eventually produced some of the most beautifully articulated of Graves' designs, as they moved in their preparatory studies this way and that off two diagonally opposite corners of the main block, eaten away at the intersection as if by their own movement, and then at last wholly detached to stand free along their diagonal axes but with eloquent voids shaped by the interaction across space between the corners of the house and themselves. The whole mass of the main block and its dependencies is gentler than that of the Plocek House. The keystone is there in the last drawings but is treated in a

planar way which has no hint of compression in it, while behind the flat frontispiece which it shapes the entrance facade steps down and opens up into two sliding planes, touched with rustication and lattice detailing to articulate the movement. A splendid model of the building exists in Graves' office. In one sense it may have found partial fulfillment in the beautiful little Bogart Beach House, which started off as all keystone, like the Plocek study, and ended up as a latticed and pergolaed block of great charm.

That whole sequence of residences, whose development was really the heart of Graves' work during these years, may be regarded as climaxing in the project for Aspen of 1978. Here the site was an ideal one, flat, at the confluence of two rivers, with the Rockies as a background. Graves' very first studies show how he hoped to respond to the mountains in plan as well as in elevation. He first shows his courtyard as deriving from the mountain like that of the Palace of Knossos from Mount Jouctas. Graves, however, inflects his court in plan to the mountain's conical shape in elevation and then draws various elevational studies of his own wherein he sets up a number of small cones, the plan responds to the rivers as well. Its center is a square court, entered exactly on axis with a monumental column on the opposite side. This also seems rather Minoan, and Graves was in fact doing drawings of the Palace of Knossos with Evans' table leg columns at about this time. From the court a pergola shoots off at a diagonal toward the pyramidal mountain, while a cross-axis opens onto one of the rivers. Its outer facade curves with the river toward another study/shrine for which there are some terrific, rather late Roman studies, recalling the "Temple of Minerva Medica" and related to Graves' work on *Roma Interrotta* and his love for Nolli's plan. This formidable monument is set out alone near the confluence of the streams, of which the angle of the second is pretty much echoed by the facade of the house on that side. The sequence of spaces is strong, even noble in plan, and is magnificently developed with enormous variety in volume and massing, especially in the earlier schemes. These propose what amounts to a little village with buildings of many different sizes and roof types but with the pyramidal shapes predominant. All of it shows a considerable family resemblance to Leon Krier's contemporary project for his school at St. Quentin-en-Ivelines. Graves' final project considerably stiffens and regularizes the building as a whole and may in some ways be regarded as a disappointment. The "preparatory studies" are full of varied life, and are again very sculpturally massive; but the "definitive drawings" are much less so. Should this be regarded as inevitable in the transformation of so protean a graphic imagination into final building form, especially into the forms of large buildings? It would not seem to be so, in this case, since the horizontal site and the lavishness of the budget might well have permitted the creation of a little village, rather than a single unified massing. In his desire for unity Graves was probably influenced by one of his more recent enthusiasms, that for the work of Joseph Hoffmann, especially for Hoffmann's narrow-pedimented classical frontispiece on the Austrian Pavilion at the Werkbund Exhibition in Cologne, of 1914. Graves adopts that tall narrow composition for his major river facade; it is attenuated in proportion—an attenuation which Hoffmann purposely accentuated by his use of flat, fluted piers rather than of columns, so creating a positively dynamic effect of thinness and vertical movement. But Graves substituted columns so tall and close together that all sense of compression is vitiated, and the whole seems an arbitrary, inactive addition to the scheme as a whole. With its insertion Graves' earlier studies lost that crouching, bouncing, gnome-like life which was their most engaging characteristic and one which was beginning to be unique to Graves' work—though up till this time to be found only, as here, in the ''preparatory studies'' for it. With the frontispiece for Aspen all this disappears and the rest of the building quiets down into a stiffly flat-topped set of cubical masses with a regularized fenestration. The effect, with the exception of Graves' log-cabin rustication (his vernacular reference, which he will use, unlike the shingles and posts of New England, because it is massive, sculptural, and primitive in its allusions), becomes strikingly Neo-Rationalist in character. Graves and Krier had, as we have noted, been associated earlier, with a possibly significant effect upon Graves, and perhaps upon Krier as well. The braced timber structure of the courtyard at Aspen strikingly resembles Krier's work, which is more static, rigorous and structural than that of Graves, based as it is on a kind of solid, pre-industrial, neo-classical vernacular. It is now significant, and perhaps a little worrying, that where Graves wanted a monumental entrance he did not transform his own keystone studies into dynamic masses, as Furness had done, but chose instead a more standard model related to Neo-Rationalism.

The changing character of Graves' historical models also suggests at least a converging relationship between his work and Neo-Rationalism at this time. As we have seen, it was the Mannerist phase of the Renaissance which seemed to attract him at first. Clearly, though, the more abstract, even heavier, threateningly sublime, rather sado-masochistic work of Claude Nicolas Ledoux had never been far in the background, and Ledoux and Boullee have always been major models for Rossi and Krier. Their influence upon Graves can only have been accentuated by the particular scholarship to which he was exposed at Princeton, like that of Josef Rykwert in eighteen-century architecture and theory. Other scholars and critics at Princeton who had always been closely associated with the New York Five, such as Anthony Vidler, have generally tended to focus upon the theory of the French Enlightenment as that most historically relevant to modern problems. Now, as with the Neo-Rationalists, that side of things comes forward in Graves' work, perhaps to the detriment of the most touching qualities it was beginning to develop, which derived not primarily from the rigorous world of French theory and structure but from the more simply physical, really more innocent Italian world of sculptural beings, each with an Cathonic life of its own.

Nevertheless, the influence of Ledoux, and perhaps even of other French work, seems to have been essential for one of Graves' most powerful projects, the monumental bridge of 1977-78 which was intended to link the two cultural centers of Fargo, North Dakota, and Moorhead, Minnesota. The first studies suggest not Palladio, as one might have expected for a classical monumental bridge, but something like Labrouste's submission to the Beaux-Arts after his years in Italy, an emblematic bridge to link Italy and France across an inconsequential stream. Graves saw Labrouste's powerful perspective for this project in Arthur Drexler's epoch-making exhibition of Beaux-Arts drawings at the Museum of Modern Art in 1975. Soon, however, pyramidal and obelisk-like shapes, suggestive once more of Mannerist garden ornaments, begin to rise in Graves' scheme. Finally, Ledoux takes over, with an amalgam of his project for a Director's House on the River Loue with the striking version of the traditional Mannerist ''Freezing-Water'' oculus that he employed in the Royal Saltworks at Arc-en-Senans. Now the scale becomes overpowering, in the Romantic-Classical way, and the segments of arches swing like great waterwheels, perversely placed at right angles to the river flow. In this a rather welcome mechanical element enters the imagery of broken arches and absent keystones. That impression is reinforced if one looks at the models of the bridge in perspective, as one would drive across it. In this view the illusionistically massive but in fact two-dimensional monumentality of the river views breaks down into a more tensile armature spanning the roadway. The effect is lighter, not only more active but also economical, so that the spectacularly sculptural whole seems somehow legitimized. It is unfortunate that a group of local business people did not think so and managed to block construction of the bridge as too extravagant for the times. Now, however, it may be revived, and Graves has already redesigned one of the cultural centers beside it, that on the Moorhead side. His first designs for these two buildings caused them to work as strong framing shapes for the bridge, pulled into a dynamic horizontal continuity with it. The present design stiffens up the earlier drawings into a unity a bit like that of Aspen but now with a certain Early Christian feeling to it (a thinned-out Rome). The planning of this building has been consistently interesting at all its stages, combining a strongly Beaux-Arts crossing of axes and unfolding of spaces with a pronounced pull to the outdoors; it now takes on a pronouncedly basilican cast. The Early Christian impression of the new massing derives in part from this.

It is important to remember that up until the last year or two it was the beautiful drawings of the bridge, in their muted, haunting colors, that represented Graves' most impressive work to date. It was this strange and compelling monument, so apparently un-modern in every way, that seemed to characterize Graves as a supremely post-modern architect, whatever that term might be taken to mean. Still, the bridge was not built, perhaps never would be, and Graves' drawings themselves had to stand for his architectural vision. They did so very well, but since they were not buildings many doubts about Graves as an architect remained. True enough, the bridge found a minor echo in the studio addition to the Abraham House in Princeton. This is now very close to completion, and the arched and keystoned motif which was most reminiscent of the bridge has been eliminated, so that the effect is a little less of a seated, rather Egyptian figure than it had originally promised to be—and it is also utterly weightless, devoid of compressive mass.

Throughout the last years of the seventies, however, Graves' titanic struggle with the keystone was never entirely abandoned. It shaped the facade of his project for French and Company, of 1978, and since these were preparatory sketches they were all compression and flourish, solid weighing upon void. Furness' Provident Trust was again recalled more closely than any of the built projects or definitive drawings had yet done. But another element is also present in the drawings, an anthropomorphic one, that too built into the classic tradition of form. So the facade, too squat to be made to look like a whole figure, is made to resemble a face, a mask. It grins and grimaces; Graves draws the shadows so that sly little eyes seem to roll*. Such facial effects, though only suggested by classical symmetries, have by no means remained unexploited in past architectures, especially from the Mannerist period onward. Richardson, Bruce Price, Maybeck, Wright, Le Corbusier, and

---

*Graves sketches sometimes recall, and Graves himself admires, Winsor McCay's dream architecture in his astounding comic strips of the early days of the century. cf Winsor McCay, Little Nemo in Slumberland, 1905-1910, Garzanti, 1969.

many others have all experimented with them at one time or another, and they are built, though normally only as leit-motifs, into any empathetic approach to design. We have noted how Graves had always used the figural reference boldly in his sketches and how at least its ghost had formed one of the complex "representations" in his work. Now it was joined by the mask, and the two studied together made it possible for him to shape his most important building, now approaching completion, the Public Service Building for Portland, Oregon. The history of this mythic structure up till now has already been well told. It is like a boy's adventure story, better than life: how it won the competition because the jury loved it and because it was also much more spacious and economical than any of the other entries; how a number of modern architects who were more or less connected with Portland acted like real bad guys, like the Beaux-Arts architects who were castigated by their idol, Sigfried Giedion, long ago, for attempting to block the construction of modern buildings*, and forced another competition; and how it won that one too for the same reasons, but how the architect had to promise to remove some of its decoration such as a gigantic piece of monumental sculpture (Portlandia) and fiberglass swags at colossal scale and a whole Early Christian settlement on the roof (that, too, suggestive of Krier's St. Quentin-en-Ivelines); and how it went into construction very fast and economically (the job captain a young woman just out of school who had never in any way been involved with a building before), and how the city fathers, full of praise, gave everything back, all the swags and the Early Christians, and are now running a competition for the figural sculpture of Portlandia, since this competition turned out so well.

All of this happened in no time at all, but time enough for everyone to see what a magnificent building this is. It is now sheathed enough so that we can see how beautifully it is set as a solid monumental block at the end of its civic garden, to be seen in splendid perspective from the bridges across the river with the hills behind it: a spectacular setting which it does everything necessary to enhance. We can see, too, how well it gets along with its older, more classical neighbors, and how it puts to shame the civic inadequacies of the neighboring curtain wall and mirror glass buldings, but to which, in the contained mirrors of its midsection, it also refers. It is thus wholly contextual, as Graves' early work, such as the Benacceraf House, was wholly not. In this, too, it abandons the International Style, with its contempt for the American downtown, which had produced several of the more inappropriate buildings nearby, those least characteristic of traditional Portland. One of the things about this building which aroused the ire of some of the designers of the others was the fact that Graves had shown a sheet of some of his study sketches for the exterior of the design. He seemed to offer numerous alternatives for its massing, and his critics sternly insisted, in the pseudo-scientific International Style manner, that there could be only one "solution" for any "problem". This reduction of art to problem solving with a single answer has been one of the more unrealistic and destructive of semi-modern tenets. But Graves' series of drawings really do build to a kind of se-

quence, a sequence of the figure and the mask. In the first sketches he tries to work it out in terms of a standing anthropomorphic shape: head, broad shoulders, toes gripping the ground. One gets fond of this group; each is a lively individual; some roll their eyes. But in the end the proportions demanded by the program don't seem to work out too well for a standing figure, so Graves makes it crouch. The head broadens back down into the mass and is maned. The knees bend, the toes become claws and clutch. Guardian lions result, all haunches, shoulders, and deep-set eyes. One great one, richly whiskered, rises back up, but compression is being transmitted all down his body as in one of the Furness' bank facades. But finally all of that must have begun to look too over-articulated, and it was felt that the whole had to be pulled into a simpler profile and more abstract image in order to become a reasonable building proposition. Now the squatness and broadness which were built into the required cubage if it were to be constructed economically suggest the final image, which is that of a mask. The crouching figure still lurks there, its toes seizing the ground, but the face has taken over the body. Under its noble keystone-forehead it looks out at us with two round eyes. The compression suggested by the keystone, though extremely restrained, also works in directly physical as well as associational terms. It pushes down through the middle of the block, exerting a visual weight upon the monumental piers which then transmit it downward to the ground-story's grip on the earth. This is so forceful that we hardly notice that it is all contained in a regular, flat, square-windowed shell.

Looked at in a related way, the flattenings and planar simplification, combined with the building's blocky, symmetrical mass, make it look very much like Art Deco. And Art Deco has been of interest to Graves for many years, as it has to Venturi. But considered more integrally, in terms of its process of design, the building is essentially Sullivanian. Its general size and proportion put it more or less in the Wainwright class. Both Sullivan and Graves were attempting to clad a light steel skeleton in order to transform it into an integral plastic body. Sullivan employs a flat, sharply cut base. So does Graves. Sullivan then sets a building-scaled panel of vertical piers within the containing flat frames of the building's corners. The capitals of the piers make them seem to support the top floor as one horizontal shape, which is treated as a great entablature for the building as a whole. Graves uses the piers only in the center and causes the corner sheathing, now with necessary but minimal and totally scaleless fenestration, to expand over more of the surface, so making the building seem a more decisively solid block if one much less richly articulated by substantial vertical piers. There is in effect no continuous entablature, no giant capital in terms of Sullivan's imagery of the classical column, but the spread of the keystone takes our attention away from that fact as well, while the horizontal planes of the village on the roof, along with its projecting corbels, help to terminate the mass and to sanction its flat top by populating it. Once again, though, if we look back beyond Sullivan to the architect for whom, as a young man, Sullivan had decided that he would work because that architect was "making buildings up out of his head"—back, that is, to Furness—we find that Graves is at least working in harmony with his major precursor. The program itself has caused him to trust in a simpler and more powerful physical bulk, less compromised by pictorial signs and surface "representation". Even the swags floating in the wind (seeming, of course, to float) play a part in this. In classical architecture swags and so on are normally carved in relief, but here they are brought out into three dimensions, so completely reversing Graves' earlier and perhaps still general tendency to flatten and pictorialize his sources.

But if we look more deeply yet we can realize how much Graves and Furness really share. They are both American architects who turn to European originals for their inspiration. With those they each do a similar thing: they take a part to make the whole; they blow up the scale; they assume European shapes and use them in the most unexpected and academically "incorrect" combinations. Out of this process Furness created forms which were barbarously strong, as brutal as machines when compared with their European prototypes. Graves has been, as we have seen, more evocative, less powerful—not physically energetic like Furness and his age, but a little sad, like ours, attuned to theatrical optical effects and illusion. But curiously, too, the center of inspiration has been fundamentally classical for both of them. For Furness it was the special French machine-age classicism of the Neo-Grec, as it was allied through Labrouste and Viollet-le-duc with the actively structural, materialistically oriented French Gothic revival of the same period. For Graves, as we have seen, it has been less France than Italy, and Mannerism's unquiet garden where the Titans crouch among the stones. His classicism, like Furness', is thus a fundamentally primitive, figurally active one of the giant in the building, and it may be said to exist in tension with his scenographic bent and perhaps to have been generally dominated by it. Indeed, that captive giant has so far been released only in sketches and, to an important degree, in Portland, but it distinguishes his work absolutely from the static, fixed, non-figural neo-classicism of the Neo-Rationalist Europeans—however much their simplified, beautifully constructed forms may appeal to Graves, as they do to us all. His tradition, despite himself, is in part a different one. It grows out of the vulgar vitality of the nineteenth century and, however much it may want to do so, it cannot, like the contemporary Europeans, disown it utterly in favor of a pure, pre-industrial, eighteenth-century order. Therefore, despite his Tuscan villa, and whether or not he refuses to value the vernacular or will ever grow to an interest in American architecture comparable to that he feels for European, Graves is in some measurable degree an American architect with roots in its nineteenth-century tradition.

There are indications that an increased awareness of his debt to that tradition may be essential to the continued vitality of Graves' work. The issue may well be joined at the present time. So the beautiful project for the Public Library at San Juan Capistrano, with its Krier-like pier groups and tight gables, may be a little less layered with action and allusion, and a bit more Neo-Rationalized and Early Christianized than any of Graves' earlier projects were. Some of its lively details, it is true, seem more purely Hispanic, or perhaps once again pre-Columbian in origin. Can their density and energy be transferred to a building of considerable size? Furness surely wrestled with that challenge. We have seen that it could be done in a primarily vertical (hence empathetically anthropomorphic) block—like those in Portland and Philadelphia. Perhaps the Education Center for New Jersey poses the problem most clearly. The little windmills, strung out to receive the breeze from the bay, are among Graves' most delightful creatures, while the building is an exceptionally fine Early Christian Basilica, in plan as well as massing. It is a useful, gentle, spatial, and directly structural type. One can go a long way with it, but, like original Early Christian architecture before it, it gives up the pagan sculptural image which populated antiquity with gods and which returned with the Renaissance and has been

employed by Graves to haunt, at Portland even to enliven, our all-too-lifeless world. Losing this, the building loses its residue of, perhaps only its reference to, energetic physicality. It should be remembered that Furness himself lost much of his own under the influence of the magisterial continuities of Richardson's design. Now the lure—a real one—is the fixed typological order of the Neo-Rationalists' work. They, like all Europeans, have the closed garden of Augustan classicism to retire into whenever, as in this generation, they feel the need to do so, and it is true that the classic image and classic order have been equally sympathetic to American artists as well. But the garden of America is also without walls. The American artist treads a kind of wilderness. It leads him toward monstrous growths which do not suggest themselves to Europeans; the skyscraper itself was one.

Furness' buildings were of that character; they wilfully misread the order of Europe and so tapped special sources of energy of a kind which have so far only been touched—but palpably, prophetically touched by the work of Graves. That work is unique in the world at present and nothing about it is yet decided. The swags will soon be flying in Portland, and then we'll see.

Vincent Scully, June, 1981

Now, a year later, having seen the Portland building on its site, one can hardly do other than to regard it as a solid vindication of Graves' method of design. We now see that the issue is a contextual one, and that Graves has scored a significant triumph in that regard. The building is of Portland and for Portland, a victory of mind and spirit in this place. Now the question of compression, for example, no longer seems to pose a serious problem. The piers and the keystone do not seem to be too thin, because their visual movement is so definitely up, not down, as one approaches and enters the building. It lifts overhead in a spreading surface display. The effect is generous, triumphant. The issue is no longer one of mass. The mass is clear enough, and exactly in accord with that of the buildings beside it. The surface expands across it, giving life to the whole without demeaning the adjacent buildings. At the same time, the deeply recessed loggia behind the flat piers of the ground floor offers an alternate route around the building but is contained within its envelope. Hence the mass is clearly seen as containing an ample volume. Straight ahead, the major entrance axis is restricted in size and is decorated by Graves in a way that makes it seem the very soul of a traditional municipal lobby. There is a touching sense of familiarity, even of a totally unexpected cultural assurance. The interior thus has an iconographic dimension, one which is deeply nourished by some of the most commonly shared experiences of our urbanistic past.

One is at home there, as one had never again expected to be in a modern office building. It is neither reductive nor alientating in its effect. The eye slides over nothing. Everything is singular, important, a little dark, and not very large. It all celebrates the decent penury of municipal space, in shocking contrast to the empty luxuries of the commercial office buildings round about it. It makes one proud to be decently poor; the word "citizen" takes on a special physical credibility. In this way the building brings some not-so-old but almost forgotten American traditions to life. To that end Graves carefully studied the heart of downtown Portland as it was before it was struck by the International Style. His colors are equivalents of those of the fine old buildings which are now being restored and rehabilitated in that rich, dense, center. His own building is therefore playing a central role in the revival of an especially sympathetic downtown area, which Portland's emphatically is. So its piers and tondi all find their echoes in adjacent buildings. The final state of the swags, which were made flat in response to the client's request to be able to clean the windows from the outside, may be a little regretted, especially as they obscure the circle of the tondi on those sides. They now float tightly past the building like a band of Art-Deco clouds. The fact that the mirror glass is only a cladding and does not affect the illumination of the interior, which is entirely by square windows, may also be regrettable. From across the river, the loss of the village on the roof (to which in the end Graves reluctantly agreed for reasons of economy) seems especially to be deplored. There the building is seen against the backdrop of Portland's wonderful bluffs, packed with houses among their trees. Graves' village would have seemed to call to them; it, too, was a marvellously contextual idea. Even so, his building takes its place perfectly in Portland's solid grid between the river and the hills. By any reasonable definition of the term, it is an entirely modern building, finding new "objective correlatives" for every one of the great, traditional shapes which it employs, and reproducing none of them. Because of that it should be taken as a major and highly creative step toward the salvation of our cities from the mindless junk with which they have recently been strewn. It enhances the meaning and enlarges the emotional scope of the office building program, and as such it touches the very heart of the city, the place where we work. But it belongs to town government most of all and is a monument to the principle of civic pride. When the mighty figure of Portlandia eventually takes her place at gigantic scale above the entrance that iconography will be complete. At one stroke, everything lost has returned, the monumental community building and its colossal figural sculpture: the human environment and the human act together.

Vincent Scully, June, 1982

298

AWARDS

PRIX DE ROME, American Academy in Rome 1960-1962

ARNOLD W. BRUNNER FELLOWSHIP, American Academy in Rome 1960-1962

FELLOW, American Institute of Architects 1979

ARNOLD W. BRUNNER MEMORIAL PRIZE IN ARCHITECTURE,
American Academy and Institute of Arts and Letters 1980

AMERICAN INSTITUTE OF ARCHITECTS, NATIONAL HONOR AWARDS:
Hanselmann House 1975
Gunwyn Ventures, Investment Office.................................1979
Schulman House...1982

NEW JERSEY SOCIETY OF ARCHITECTS, A.I.A. AWARDS:
Oyster Bay Town Plan 1967
Hanselmann House 1973
Union County Nature and Science Museum 1974
Alexander House..1975
E.N.T. Medical Offices..1975
Snyderman House..1976
Crooks House 1976
Warehouse Conversion: Private Residence 1977
House in Aspen, Colorado 1978
Schulman House...1978
Abrahams Dance Studio 1978
Fargo-Moorhead Cultural Center Bridge 1978
Sunar Furniture Showroom, New York 1979
Sunar Furniture Showroom, Houston 1980
New Jersey Railroad Station 1980
Environmental Education Center 1980
San Juan Capistrano Public Library 1981
Sunar Furniture Showroom, New York 1981

PROGRESSIVE ARCHITECTURE DESIGN AWARDS:
Rockefeller House...1970
Snyderman House...1975
Crooks House 1977
Chem-Fleur Factory Addition and Renovation 1978
Warehouse Conversion: Private Residence 1978
Fargo-Moorhead Cultural Center Bridge 1979
Plocek House 1980
Kalko House 1980
Beach House 1980

INTERIORS MAGAZINE:
Designer of the Year 1980
Sunar Furniture Showroom, New York 1981

SELECTED WRITINGS ON MICHAEL GRAVES

1966
ROBERT A.M. STERN, *The Jersey Corridor Project*, in ''40 Under 40'', The Architectural League of New York, 1966.

1967
The New City: Architecture and Urban Renewal, Museum of Modern Art, New York, 1967.

1968
Architecture of Museums, Museum of Modern Art, New York, 1968.

1970
14th Annual Design Awards, *Private Residence, Pocantico Hills, New York*, in ''Progressive Architecture'' v. 51, January 1970.

1972
Five Architects, Eisenman, Graves, Gwathmey, Hejduk, Meier, Wittenborn & Co., New York, 1972. Oxford University Press, New York, 1975.

MARIO GANDELSONAS, *On Reading Architecture*, cover design, in ''Progressive Architecture'' v. 53, March 1972.

1973
PETER CARL, *Towards a Pluralist Architecture*, in ''Progressive Architecture'' v. 54, February 1973.

Five on Five: ROBERT A. M. STERN, *Stompin' at the Savoye;* JAQUELIN ROBERTSON, *Machines in the Garden;* CHARLES MOORE, *In Similar State of Undress;* ALLEN GREENBERG, *The Lurking American Legacy*, ROMALDO GIURGOLA, *The Discreet Charm of the Bourgeoisie*, cover, in ''The Architectural Forum'' v. 138, May 1973.

PETER PAPADEMETRIOU, *Architecture*, in ''Architectural Design'' v. 43, November 1973.

PAUL GOLDBERGER, *Architecture's Big Five Elevate Form*, in ''The New York Times'', November 26, 1973.

Projects at the XV Triennale, in ''Architettura Razionale'', Edited by E. BONFANTI, R. BONICALZI, A. ROSSI, M. SCOLARI & D. VITALE, Angeli Editore, Milan, 1973.

Esposizione Internationale delle Arti Decorative e Industriali Moderne e dell' Architettura Moderna, XV Triennale di Milano, November 1973.

1974
PAUL GOLDBERGER, *Should Anyone Care About the 'New York Five'?*, in ''Architectural Record'' v. 155, February 1974.

MANFREDO TAFURI, *L'architecture dans le Boudoir*, in ''Oppositions'' n. 3, May 1974.

Benacerraf House, Hanselmann House, Alexander House, in ''Global Interiors 6, Houses in USA'', A.D.A. EDITA Tokyo, 1974.

C. RAY SMITH, Editorial, *Painterly Illusion and Architectural Reality*, in ''Interiors'' v. 134, September 1974.

1975
KENNETH FRAMPTON, *Five Architects*, in ''Lotus International'' n. 9, February 1975.

SUZANNE STEPHENS, *Semantic Distinctions*, in ''Progressive Architecture'' v. 56, April 1975.

Honor Awards 1975. *Hanselmann Residence*, in ''AIA Journal'' v. 63, May 1975.

JOHN MAULE McKEAN, *The Architect as Intellectual Artist*, in ''Building Design'', October 10, 1975.

1976
23rd Annual Design Awards, *Snyderman House*, in ''Progressive Architecture'' v. 57, January 1976.

C. RAY SMITH, *Layers of Space and Symbol*, in ''The New York Times Magazine, The Home'', September 26, 1976.

MANFREDO TAFURI: *American Graffiti: Five X Five = Twenty-five*, in ''Oppositions'' n. 5, Summer 1976.

YVONNE DEAN, *The Famous Five, A Literary Exploration*, and ALAN COLQUHOUN, *New York Five, an English Reply*, in ''Art Net'' n. 2, 1976.

ALISON SKY & MICHELE STONE, *Unbuilt America*, McGraw-Hill, New York, 1976.

MANFREDO TAFURI, *Five Architects N.Y.*, Officina Edizioni, Rome, 1976.

1977

24th Annual Design Awards, *Crooks House*, in "Progressive Architecture" v. 58, January 1977.

CHARLES JENCKS, *The Language of Post-Modern Architecture*, Academy Editions, London, 1977.

DAVID GEBHARD & DEBORAH NEVINS, *200 Years of American Architectural Drawing*, Watson-Guptill, New York, 1977.

ROBERT A.M. STERN, *New Directions in American Architecture*, George Braziller, New York, 1977.

1978

25th Annual Design Awards, *Chem-Fleur Factory Addition and Renovation*, and *Warehouse Conversion: Private Residence*, in "Progressive Architecture" v. 59, January 1978.

Michael Graves: Benacerraf House, in "Architectural Design" v. 48, January 1978.

RICHARD POMMER, *Architecture: Structures for the Imagination*, in "Art in America" v. 66, March/April 1978.

SUZANNE STEPHENS, *Living in a Work of Art*, cover, in "Progressive Architecture" v. 59, March 1978.

Color from the Outside In, in "House and Garden" v. 150, September 1978.

Michael Graves: Claghorn House Addition, in "G.A. Houses 5", A.D.A. EDITA Tokyo, 1978.

CHARLES JENCKS, *Late Modernism and Post-Modernism*, in "Architectural Design" v. 48, December 1978.

1979

26th Annual Design Awards, *Fargo-Moorhead Cultural Center Bridge*, in "Progressive Architecture" v. 60, January 1979.

WILLIAM MARLIN, *Prairie Cultural Causeway a Dream Bridge*, in "The Christian Science Monitor", April 27, 1979.

PAUL GOLDBERGER, *Architecture: Works of Michael Graves*, in "The New York Times", May 11, 1979.

M.E. OSMAN, 1979 AIA Honor Awards, *Creating A New And Colorful Interior Work*, in "AIA Journal" v. 68, mid-May 1979.

ADA LOUISE HUXTABLE, *A Unified New Language of Design*, in "The New York Times", May 27, 1979.

ROSEMARIE HAAG BLETTER, *About Graves*, in "Skyline", Summer 1979.

MARTIN FILLER, *Grand Allusions*, in "Progressive Architecture" v. 60, June 1979.

MARTIN FILLER, *Better and Better*, cover design, in "Progressive Architecture" v. 60, September 1979.

The Power of Color, in "The New York Times Magazine, Home Design", September 30, 1979.

PHILIP SMITH, *Graves's New World*, in "Gentlemen's Quarterly" v. 49, November 1979.

CAROL FELDER, *Architecture, Anyone?*, in "New Jersey Monthly" v. 4, November 1979.

VINCENT SCULLY, *Vincent Scully on the Michael Graves Monograph*, in "Architectural Design" v. 49, October/November 1979.

DEBORAH NEVINS & ROBERT A.M. STERN, *The Architect's Eye*, Pantheon, New York, 1979.

EDIE COHEN, *Sunar, Chicago*, cover, in "Interior Design" v. 50, December 1979.

ARTHUR DREXLER, *Transformations in Modern Architecture*, Museum of Modern Art, New York, 1979.

ALAN COLQUHOUN, *From Bricolage to Myth: or How to Put Humpty-Dumpty Together Again*, in "oppositions" n. 12, Spring 1978 (publ. 1979).

PETER EISENMAN, *The Graves of Modernism*, in "Oppositions" n. 12, Spring 1978 (publ. 1979)

Michael Graves, Architectural Monographs, Edited by DAVID DUNSTER, Academy Editions, London, 1979.

1980

PILAR VILADAS, *Cutting up the Rug*, in "Interiors" v. 139, January 1980.

27th Annual Design Awards, *Kalko House, Green Brook, N.J.*; *Plocek House, Warren, N.J.*; *Beach House, Loveladies, N.J.*, in "Progressive Architecture" v. 61, January 1980.

RICHARD HORN, *Connecting with Color*, in "Residential Interiors" v. 5, January 1980.

MARTIN FILLER, *The Man Who's Rewriting the Language of Color*, in "House & Garden" v. 152, March 1980.

CHARLES JENCKS, *Late-Modern Architecture*, Rizzoli International, New York, 1980.

Snyderman House, in "GA Document Special Issue, 1970-1980", A.D.A. EDITA Tokyo, 1980.

CHARLES K. GANDEE, *Sunar Houston: The Allusive Language of Michael Graves*, in "Architectural Record" v. 168, June 1980.

ELENI CONSTANTINE, *The Case for Michael Graves's Design for Portland*, cover, in ''Architectural Record'' v. 168, August 1980.

DOUGLAS DAVIS, *Building with Symbols*, in ''Newsweek'', September 1, 1980.

MARTIN FILLER, *Michael Graves: Before and After*, in ''Art in America'' v. 68, September 1980.

CHARLES JENCKS, *Post-Modern Classicism: Introduction, Sunar Showroom, Plocek House, Portland Building*, in ''Architectural Design'' v. 50.

ADA LOUISE HUXTABLE, *The Boom in Bigness Goes on*, in ''The New York Times'', December 28, 1980.

1981

PILAR VILADAS, *Michael Graves: Designer of the Year*, cover, in ''Interiors'' v. 140, January 1981.

JUDITH TURNER, *Judith Turner Photographs Five Architects*, Rizzoli International, New York, 1981.

San Juan Capistrano Library Design Competition, in ''Architectural Record'' v. 169, March 1981.

ADA LOUISE HUXTABLE, *Architecture at the Crossroads*, cover, in ''Dialogue'' n. 53, March 1981.

CYNTHIA SALTZMAN, *Architect Michael Graves: Changing the Horizon''*, in ''The Wall Street Journal'', May 1, 1981.

NORY MILLER, *Full Circle*, in ''Progressive Architecture'' v. 62, August 1981.

TOM WOLFE, *From Bauhaus To Our House*, Farrar Straus Giroux, New York, 1981.

ROBERT SAM ANSON, *Michael Graves: The Rise of the Architect-Poet*, in ''Metropolitan Home'' v. 13, November 1981.

Architecture and Vegetal Inclusions, in ''Lotus International'' n. 31, 1981.

SELECTED WRITINGS AND INTERVIEWS OF MICHAEL GRAVES

1975

(With CAROLINE CONSTANT) *The Swedish Connection*, in ''Journal of Architectural Education'' v. 29, September 1975.

1977

(With M. PERKINS) *Michael Graves: Snyderman House*, in ''G.A. Houses 2'', A.D.A. EDITA Tokyo, 1977.

(With others) *Elusive Outcome, Mental Mise-en-scene*, in ''Progressive Architecture'' v. 58, May 1977.

The Necessity of Drawing: Tangible Speculation, in ''Architectural Design'' v. 47, June 1977.

1978

Porta Maggiore, in ''Roma Interrotta'', Incontri Internazionali d'Arte, Rome, 1978.

(Interview with DOUGLAS ELY) *Toward Reading an Architecture; an interview with Michael Graves*, in ''Nassau Literary Review'', Princeton University, Spring 1978.

Thought Models, in ''Great Models'', North Carolina State University School of Design, Fall 1978.

Referential Drawings, in ''Journal of Architectural Education'' v. 32, September 1978.

(With PETER BOHLIN & HUGH HARDY) *Three Architects, Three Approaches to Color Use*, in ''AIA Journal'' v. 67, October 1978.

1979

Roma Interrotta: Guest Editor, cover design, *Roman Interventions*, and *Nolli Sector IX, Porta Maggiore*, in ''Architectural Design'' v. 49, March 1979.

Referential Design: Vacation House in Aspen, Colorado, in ''International Architect'' v. 1, 1979.

Michael Graves, in ''Buildings for Best Products'', Edited by ARTHUR DREXLER, Museum of Modern Art, New York, 1979.

1980

(Interview with PHILIP SMITH) *Michael Graves: A Modern Architect*, in ''Arts Magazine'' v. 54, April 1980.

(Interview with ASHLEY E. HARVIE) *Post Modern Expressions: An Interview with Michael Graves*, in ''The Designer'' v. 21, New York, May 1980.

The Value of Color, in ''Architectural Record'' v. 168, June 1980.

(Interview with BARBARALEE DIAMONSTEIN) *Michael Graves*, in *American Architecture Now*, Rizzoli International, New York, 1980.

(Interview with MARK A. HEWITT, BENJAMIN KRACAUER, JOHN MASSENGALE & MICHAEL McDONOUGH) *An Interview with Michael Graves*, in ''Via'' v. 4, University of Pennsylvania, 1980.

(With GARY WOLF) *Beyond Mere Manners and Cosmetic Compatibility*, in *Old and New Architec-*

ture, *Design Relationship*, National Trust for Historic Preservation, Washington, 1980.

(Interview with ABRAHAM ROGATNICK) *An Interview with Michael Graves*, in ''Forum'' n. 9, Vancouver, September 1980.

1981

Michael Graves, in ''The Presence of the Past'', Edited by GABRIELLA BORSANO, Venice Biennale and Electa Editrice, Milan, 1981.

Thoughts on Furniture, in ''Furniture by Architects'', Massachusetts Institute of Technology, 1981.

Michael Graves, in ''Speaking a New Classicism: American Architecture Now'', Smith College Museum of Art, Northampton, Massachusetts, 1981.

(Seminar) *Michael Graves*, in ''Yale Seminars in Architecture'' v. 1, Edited by CESAR PELLI, Yale University, 1981.

(Interview, Michael Graves and Joe d'Urso), *Perspectives from the East*, in ''Designers West'' v. 28, May 1981.

(Interview with IAIN BLAIR) *Michael Graves, an Interview with Iain Blair*, in ''Revue'' v. 2, Los Angeles, Summer 1981.

(Interview with CARL MOMBERG et al.) *Michael*

Graves, cover, in ''Architecture SA'', South Africa, August 1981.

(Interview with WILSON HAND KIDDE & LARZ FERGUSON ANDERSON) *Michael Graves Builds His Reputation*, in ''Interview'' v. 11, September 1981.

(Interview with JOANNA CENCI RODRIGUEZ) *Interview with Michael Graves*, in ''Florida Architect'' v. 28, Fall 1981.

(With LENNART ANDERSON) *Bacchanal*, in ''Collaboration, Artists and Architects'', Edited by BARBARALEE DIAMONSTEIN, Whitney Library of Design, New York, 1981.

Le Corbusier's Drawn References, in *Le Corbusier: Selected Drawings*, Academy Editions, London, 1981.

The Wageman House and the Crooks House, cover, in ''Idea as Model'' cat. 3, Institute for Architecture and Urban Studies and Rizzoli International, 1981.

(Interview with MICHAEL McTWIGAN) *What is the Focus of Post-Modern Architecture? An Interview with Michael Graves*, in ''American Artist'' v. 45, December 1981.

Michael Graves, in *Architectural Drawing: The Art and the Process*, by GERALD ALLEN and RICHARD OLIVER, Whitney Library of Design, New York,